How to Achieve Legal Success in the United States

How to Achieve Legal Success in the United States

A Survival Guide for Foreign Attorneys

Maike M. Lara Espinal, LL.M.

DEDICATION

To all international lawyers who seek a better future and a place in the global legal community, especially those who face challenges with courage and determination.

ACKNOWLEDGMENTS

To my family, there are not enough words to express my gratitude. Thank you for making immeasurable sacrifices to provide me with a quality education and always being by my side with unwavering support and unconditional love. Your efforts, big and small, have been the foundation upon which I have built my dreams and goals. Without you, none of this would have been possible.

To Kevin, my rock since we met three years ago. Your unwavering support and constant love have been my beacon during the LL.M. journey and the creation of this book. Thank you for being there every step of the way, listening patiently, and offering valuable revisions and feedback. Your presence has made every challenge more bearable and every success sweeter.

To my dear friends, Linda and Aylin, who, from day one, became my favorite study group and emotional support. Your laughter, advice, and shoulders to lean on have been crucial on this journey. I also want to thank my other LL.M. classmates whose support and camaraderie made this process enriching and memorable. Special thanks to Mohammed who has helped me to review the Arabic version of this book.

To all the professors and staff at St. John's University School of Law, from whom I had the privilege of learning, your teachings and guidance have left an indelible mark on my professional and personal development. Special thanks to Professor Paras for always being an unwavering support and for your invaluable bar exam preparation. Also, thanks to Professor Cole for agreeing to write the foreword of this book and for constantly inspiring me as a former LL.M. student now guiding new generations.

Likewise, I am grateful to Professor McGuiness for welcoming me as a research assistant and expanding my interest in international law with your vast knowledge. Finally, I thank Professor Olson for all your support in the application process and help understanding program requirements.

To my undergraduate professors at Universidad Iberoamericana, your dedication and support have been fundamental in my academic development. Special thanks to Professor Sagrario Féliz de Cochon, who has been a guide and exceptional support since our first encounter in high school, especially during this dual degree process.

Likewise, to my first teachers at the Centro de Cuidado y Desarrollo del Niño and the Colegio Calasanz. Thank you for believing in my potential from my earliest steps, instilling solid values, and planting the seeds of professionalism that have flourished throughout my academic and professional journey. Your faith in me and dedication have been essential for obtaining my LL.M. and producing this book.

Finally, I sincerely appreciate the friends that life has gifted me and who have been remarkable in this process. Each of you has brought something unique and valuable to my life. Your words of encouragement, company under challenging times, and shared laughter have been fundamental pillars for me. Your friendship has made this journey more bearable and meaningful; I will be eternally grateful for that.

TABLE OF CONTENTS

FOREWORD

As a student who embarked on the journey of legal studies overseas, Maike quickly realized that this experience is far more than just an academic pursuit; it is a profound life transformation. At 25, Maike found himself navigating the intricate maze of law school, campus life, and the challenges of adapting to a new environment far from home. His passion for writing and helping others drove him to share this journey, not just as a narrative of his own experiences, but as a guide for those who will follow in his footsteps.

This book is born out of Maike's desire to give back to a community that has shaped him in ways he never imagined. Utilizing his language advantages, Maike has prepared this book in Spanish, English, French, and Chinese, ensuring that it reaches and resonates with a diverse group of students from around the world. He believes that every student entering an LLM program, whether fresh out of undergraduate studies or stepping into it with professional experience, carries with them the potential to make a significant impact. However, the path is not always clear, and the challenges can sometimes seem insurmountable. This book is his attempt to demystify that path, offering insights not just into surviving the academic rigors of an LLM program but thriving in all aspects of this unique journey.

As his law school professor, and as someone who graduated from the same LLM program, I am deeply inspired by Maike's dedication. Not only has he pushed himself to reach the highest levels of professional excellence, but he has also put his thoughts into practice in a way that helps others—not just his peers, but also those he may never meet. This kind of strong leadership is exactly what society needs today: leaders who break down barriers, advocate for the underserved, fight for what seems impossible, and set a higher bar for others to aspire to.

Throughout these pages, you will find practical advice on how to maximize your time both on and off campus. From mastering coursework to preparing for the bar exam, from building a professional network to finding meaningful employment post-graduation, Maike's aim is to provide you with the tools and strategies that have proven invaluable to him and many others. He knows firsthand how a small idea can grow into something that has the power to transform lives. The challenges you will face are real, but so too is the support and knowledge that can be gained through shared experiences.

Maike hopes this book serves not just as a guide, but as a companion, offering encouragement and practical wisdom as you navigate this exciting and challenging chapter of your life. May it inspire you to pursue your goals with determination and to help those who come after you, just as he has been inspired to help you.

Welcome to this journey. Your adventure begins now.

Chunxia Cole, Esq.
Adjunct Professor
St. John's University School of Law

INTRODUCTION

E ntering the legal sector of another country can seem like a daunting challenge, and indeed it is, but this should not be a limitation to embarking on this endeavor. Globalization and the increasing interconnection between countries have made the knowledge and practice of law in an international context more accessible and valuable than ever. This book is aimed at professionals and law students who wish to expand their careers to practice in the United States, one of the world's largest and most competitive legal markets.

The purpose of this book is to serve as a practical guide, offering a series of detailed steps and strategic advice so that legal professionals and students can successfully transition into the U.S. legal market. Here, you will find essential information on the administrative, academic, and professional aspects necessary to navigate and succeed in the U.S. legal system.

The United States is distinguished not only for having one of the most complex legal systems but also for being a hub of international legal practice. With its vast diversity of state and federal laws, the U.S. legal system offers unique specialization and professional development opportunities. Additionally, many multinational law firms and companies with global operations are headquartered or have significant offices in the United States, making this country an attractive destination for lawyers looking to broaden their professional horizons.

This book is organized into several key sections, each designed to address a crucial aspect of integrating into the U.S. legal system:

1. Selecting the Right Program: We will explore how to evaluate and select the academic program that best fits your professional goals, comparing programs such as the LL.M. and the J.D.

2. Applying for a Student Visa: Understand the different types of visas available, the application process, the necessary documents, and practical tips for the consular interview.

3. Let's Talk Money: We will break down the costs associated with studying and living in the United States, and explore available financing options, including scholarships and work opportunities for international students.

4. Things to Know in Advance: Prepare for academic and cultural life in the United States by highlighting key differences between the U.S. legal system and other legal systems.

5. Ethics for Law Students: We will address the importance of academic and professional ethics and how it applies in the context of legal education in the United States.

6. A Typical Day in Class: Get strategies to manage and excel in the Socratic teaching method commonly used in U.S. law schools.

7. Exams in Law School: Learn about the different types of exams, as well as effective study and preparation techniques.

8. Securing Employment: We will offer tips on how to secure internships and jobs, including networking and interview preparation.

9. Different Exams for Admission: Cover the key exams you will need to practice law in the United States, such as the Bar Exam and the MPRE, among others.

10. Testimonials from LL.M. Students: Presenting the experiences of various students who have completed an LL.M. at different universities across the country and from different regions of the world.

11. Requirements by Jurisdiction: A compendium of the specific requirements of each state for admission to the practice of law, as well as additional resources for obtaining more information.

12. Checklist Before the First Day of Classes: A comprehensive summary of all the steps you should have completed before starting classes.

13. Additional Resources: We will provide a list of recommended books, useful websites, professional organizations and associations, and support and mentoring programs.

The path to practicing law in the United States is challenging, but it is also filled with rewarding opportunities. This book will not only equip you with the knowledge necessary to overcome initial obstacles but also provide you with the tools to thrive in your legal career in the United States. Whether you are in the exploration phase or have already decided to take this important step, this guide will be your reliable companion at every stage of the process.

This book is written from my experience in legal education in the United States. During my journey, I encountered many challenges and learned valuable lessons that would have facilitated my adaptation and success if I had known them in advance. This manual seeks to share that knowledge and offer practical guidance for those following this path.

It is important to note that consular and immigration processes always depend on U.S. consular authorities and may vary according to the applicant's country of origin and individual situation. Although I describe the processes in general terms and how they are commonly carried out, each experience is unique, and this book is intended to complement official information and the personal experiences of other international students.

Join us on this journey of discovery and preparation. With dedication, preparation, and the right information, you can become a successful legal professional in the United States. Let's get started!

1

SELECTING THE RIGHT PROGRAM

C hoosing the right academic program is a crucial decision that can largely determine your success in the U.S. legal field. From selecting the right university to choosing a specific program that meets your needs, every step of this process will influence your preparation and future professional opportunities. This chapter, will explore the different types of law programs available in the United States, the factors to consider when choosing a university, and the steps necessary to complete a successful application.

Types of Law Programs

Law schools in the United States mainly offer two types of programs for legal studies: the **Juris Doctor (J.D.)** and the **Master of Laws (LL.M.)**. Each of these programs has distinct characteristics and objectives tailored to different student profiles.

The **Juris Doctor (J.D.)** program is the primary professional degree in law in the United States. This program is designed for those seeking to obtain a license to practice law in the United States. Generally, it attracts students who have completed a bachelor's degree in any discipline, usually political science, economics, among others. The J.D. is a three-year program that offers comprehensive legal training, covering both legal fundamentals and specialized areas.

J.D. students have greater flexibility to choose from a wide range of elective courses, allowing them to specialize in specific areas of law according to their professional interests. Additionally, J.D. graduates have a greater capacity to practice in any jurisdiction within the United States as long as they pass the bar exam of the corresponding state.

The J.D. curriculum includes fundamental subjects such as constitutional law, criminal law, contracts, and civil law. These subjects form the basis of legal knowledge, which will be expanded upon with elective and clinical courses that allow students to gain practical experience. Additionally, constant interaction with professors and peers, as well as participation in extracurricular activities such as moot court, law review, and research assistance enrich J.D. students educational and professional experience.

The **Master of Laws (LL.M.)** program is designed for lawyers who have obtained their law degree in another country and wish to specialize in a specific area of U.S. or international law. LL.M. programs typically last one or two years, depending on jurisdictional requirements and the program's focus.

LL.M. programs are highly specialized, allowing international lawyers to gain advanced knowledge in specific areas such as international law, commercial law, human rights, environmental law, and more. Due to the shorter duration of the program, opportunities to choose elective courses are more limited. Consequently, most of the classes are basic requirements to ensure a solid understanding of the U.S. legal system.

It is essential to verify personal priorities and goals before making a decision. Some LL.M. programs are specifically designed for students who wish to specialize in an area of law and return to their home countries to apply their knowledge. On the other hand, some programs are geared toward preparing students to practice in the United States, providing broader training focused on the U.S. legal system.

If you wish to practice in the United States, the chosen program must adequately prepare you for the bar exam, as not all LL.M. programs offer this preparation. Each state has specific requirements for international lawyers to take the bar exam. For example, some states, like New York, allow LL.M. graduates to take the exam, while others have stricter restrictions. It is essential to research the specific requirements of the jurisdiction where you plan to practice and directly contact university admissions offices for detailed information on how their LL.M. program prepares you for the bar exam.

In addition to coursework, LL.M. programs may include opportunities for internships at law firms, companies, non-governmental organizations, and government agencies. These practical experiences are invaluable for international students, as they allow them to apply their knowledge in real-world contexts and build professional networks in the United States.[1]

Choosing between a J.D. and an LL.M. program depends on your professional goals, prior academic background, and plans for practicing law in the United States. The J.D. provides broad and detailed training in U.S. law, ideal for those seeking a full license to practice in any U.S. jurisdiction. On the other hand, the LL.M. offers advanced specialization for international lawyers who wish to deepen their knowledge in specific areas of U.S. or international law. Understanding these differences will help you make an informed decision aligned with your professional goals.

Researching Programs and Universities

Choosing the right university is a critical factor in selecting the right law program. Each university offers different strengths, approaches, and opportunities that can influence your education and professional career. To make an informed decision, it is essential to consider several key aspects when researching programs and universities.

Investigating the prestige of the university and the specific program is fundamental. Universities with well-established and globally recognized law programs can offer better networking and employment opportunities. Rankings in specialized publications can provide an overview of the academic reputation of law schools. However, it is important not to base the decision solely on these rankings but also consider other factors relevant to your professional and personal goals.

Additionally, the location of the university can influence your professional opportunities and quality of life. Studying in a city with a dynamic legal market can offer more internships, jobs, and networking opportunities. Furthermore, location also affects the cost of living, access

---

[1] The U.S. News & World Report offers good comparisons between both programs, which can be accessed at https://www.usnews.com/education/articles/getting-an-llm-degree-what-to-know

to resources, and the possibility of establishing contacts in the region where you plan to practice. Some cities, such as New York, Los Angeles, and Washington D.C., are known for their extensive legal opportunities, but the cost of living is extremely high, and it is crucial to balance this.

Some universities value LL.M. students and their cultural diversity more, providing an inclusive and supportive academic environment. It is essential to identify programs that do not place LL.M. students in the background and offer full integration into the educational and extracurricular life of the university. Reviewing current student and alums testimonials can provide a useful perspective on how LL.M. students are valued and supported at a particular institution.

The cost of education in the United States is significant and varies depending on the university and program. It is crucial to evaluate the total cost of tuition and living expenses in the university's location. Additionally, it is essential to research scholarship opportunities and other forms of financial aid. Many universities offer specific scholarships for international students, and applying for these opportunities early in the admission process is vital. Considering the cost-benefit ratio of education at a particular institution will help you make a financially responsible decision. We will delve into this further in the book.

Similarly, evaluating the resources and academic support offered by the university is another crucial aspect. This includes the quality of the law library, access to legal databases, and the availability of tutoring and academic advising programs. Legal clinics and internship programs are also critical, as they provide practical experience that is invaluable for your training and professional development. Universities that offer strong academic support and resources can facilitate your adaptation to the U.S. legal system and improve your academic performance.

At the same time, it is important to consider the networking opportunities a university offers. Student associations, conferences, recruitment events, and alums networks are essential platforms for building professional relationships. In this sense, it is always good to research what types of networking events and activities the university organizes, as this will maximize your academic and professional experience.

Finally, it is essential to plan for the long term and consider how choosing a specific university and program aligns with your professional goals. This includes researching the success rates of graduates in terms of employment, salaries, and bar exam passage. Talking to alums and professionals in the field can provide a clear view of the opportunities and challenges you may face after completing your law program.

Application Process

Once you have selected the right program, the next step is to start the application process. This process can be rigorous and detailed, requiring careful preparation and the collection of several essential documents and materials.

The first step generally involves obtaining academic documents. Universities typically require official transcripts from all previous educational institutions you have attended. These transcripts must demonstrate your academic history and the fulfillment of the prerequisites for the program you are applying to. It is important to request these transcripts in advance, as the process of sending and verifying them can take time. In addition to transcripts, most applications also require personal identification documents, such as a copy of your passport. This ensures that the university has accurate and up-to-date information about your identity and citizenship.

For international students, English proficiency certification is a crucial requirement. Universities usually accept recognized exams such as the TOEFL (Test of English as a Foreign Language), IELTS (International English Language Testing System), or DET (Duolingo English Test). It is essential to achieve the minimum score required by the program you are applying to, as this demonstrates your ability to participate and understand course material.

Another important part of the application process is the writing sample. Some applications require a writing sample that demonstrates your legal writing skills. This can be an essay, a previous academic work, or a legal document you have written. The writing sample allows evaluators to determine your ability to communicate effectively and precisely in English.

Letters of recommendation are also an essential part of the application process. These letters should come from professors, employers, or professionals who can speak to your academic, professional, and personal abilities. It is advisable to choose people who know you well and can provide a detailed and positive evaluation of your skills and potential.

In addition to letters of recommendation, an updated curriculum vitae (CV) or resume containing your academic and professional experience is another common requirement. This document should highlight your achievements, skills, and relevant experiences that make you a good candidate for the program. Ensure that your CV is well-structured and error-free.

A critical part of your application is the statement of purpose. This personal essay allows you to explain your goals and motivations for studying in the specific program you are applying to. It should include your short- and long-term professional goals, why you have chosen that particular university, and how you believe the program will help you achieve your goals. The statement of purpose should be clear, concise, and well-written, demonstrating your passion and commitment to the field of law.

It should be meticulously reviewed before submission. Avoiding spelling and grammatical errors is crucial, as the quality of writing, organization, and presentation of documents constitutes the first impression evaluators will have of applicants. It is always advisable to seek help from professors or academics to review the documentation, ensuring it reflects professionalism and precision. This attention to detail not only enhances the applicant's credibility but also stands out positively among other candidates, increasing the chances of a favorable evaluation by admissions or selection committees.

After submitting your application, be prepared to provide any additional documentation the university may require. This could include interviews, further tests, or more details about your academic and professional experience. Stay in touch with admissions offices and respond promptly to any requests for additional information.

During the waiting period, it is useful to continue researching academic and professional life in the United States. This will better prepare you for the transition and help you make the most of your educational experience. Connect with current students and alums to gain insights into their experiences and tips on succeeding in the program.

Selecting the right law program is one of the most important decisions you will make in your legal career. From understanding the differences between J.D. and LL.M. programs, researching universities and their specific requirements, to preparing a solid application, each step is crucial to ensuring your future success. Take the necessary time to research and reflect on your options, and do not hesitate to seek advice and support during this process. With proper preparation, you will be able to find the program that best suits your needs and professional aspirations.

2

APPLYING FOR A STUDENT VISA

E ntering the American legal field involves a rigorous preparation process, and one of the first and most crucial steps is obtaining the appropriate student visa. Unless you are an American citizen or permanent resident, you will need a visa for long-term studies. The most commonly required student visa is the F-1 visa. Below is a detailed description of the complete process, the requirements to apply for and obtain this visa, as well as the steps to follow to ensure a smooth entry into the United States.[2]

There are two main categories of non-immigrant visas for individuals who wish to study in the United States: the F and M visas. These visas are designed to allow international students to enter the United States and participate in full-time educational programs.

1. F-1 Visa: This visa is for academic students who wish to enroll in an educational program at a university, college, seminary, conservatory, academic high school, elementary school or in a language training program. The F-1 visa allows students to enroll in programs that culminate in a degree, diploma, or certificate. To obtain this visa, your

---

[2] For more information on visa types and requirements, it is mandatory to review the State Department's website: https://travel.state.gov/content/travel/en/us-visas/study/student-visa.html

school must be authorized by the U.S. government to accept international students.

2. M-1 Visa: This visa is for vocational or non-academic students. Although it is not commonly used by law students, it is important to know about it in case it is needed for other types of training.

Requirements for the F-1 Visa

To qualify for an F-1 visa, you must meet the following criteria:

1. Be enrolled in an "academic" educational program, a language training program, or a vocational program.

2. The school must be approved by the Student and Exchange Visitor Program (SEVIS) of the Department of Homeland Security (DHS).

3. You must be enrolled as a full-time student at the institution.

4. You must be proficient in English or be enrolled in courses leading to English proficiency.

5. You must have sufficient funds to support yourself during the proposed course of study.

6. You must maintain a residence abroad that you have no intention of abandoning.

Accordingly, you must first be accepted into a study program at a U.S. university. Once accepted, you will receive a Form I-20 (Certificate of Eligibility for Nonimmigrant Student Status). This form certifies that you are eligible for F-1 student status and have sufficient funds to support yourself during your studies.

Process for the I-20 Form

Before applying for an F-1 visa at your country's embassy, you must request the university to issue a form called I-20. This document acknowledges that you have sufficient funds to cover your study period. The I-20 Form is a U.S. government document that universities use to certify that you are eligible for F-1 student status. To obtain this form, you must meet certain requirements:

1. Be or expect to be a bona fide student. This means being a genuine and good-faith student enrolled in a legitimate academic program in the United States.

2. Meet the university's admission requirements.

3. Pursue a full course of studies.

4. Demonstrate that you have sufficient funds to study and live in the United States without working illegally or suffering poverty.

Not all international students need an I-20. For example, J-1 students require a Form DS-2019, and F-2 dependents who wish to study full-time must obtain an I-20 and change their status to F-1 student. If you have another non-immigrant status in the United States, you may not need an I-20 and can attend school if the law permits.

To obtain your I-20 Form, you must be accepted into a full-time study program and demonstrate that you can cover the costs of living and studying in the United States. Reviewing the university's "Estimated Annual Financial Requirements for International Students" and calculating your annual costs is essential. This amount is what you must show you can cover for the first year of study. It is recommended to budget at least 10% more to avoid financial problems.

Financial support can come from various sources, both within and outside the United States. It is possible to have sponsors who provide you with cash support or free room and board. It is advisable that part of the financial support comes from your home country, as this is important for obtaining your student visa. Sponsors should promise only the amount of money they can realistically provide, as a common reason for visa denial is that the consular officer is not convinced the sponsor can provide the promised amount. If you have personal funds, you must demonstrate that you have enough money to cover your entire study program or have other personal income.

To demonstrate your financial capability, you must provide several documents:

- **Cash Support Sponsors** must present an annual cash support affidavit and include proof of income, such as an employer letter, tax returns, or investment documentation. If a business sponsors you, you must present the company's latest profit and loss statement and an official statement of the salary paid to the owner/sponsor.

- **Free Room and Board Sponsors** must present a free room and board affidavit and copies of documents such as the lease agreement or utility bills.

It is important not to enter the United States with a B-1, B-2, or B-1/B-2 visa if you plan to study, as this can be seen as a "fraudulent entry" and could result in denial of your status extension or change. Visitors with a B visa are prohibited from pursuing a full course of study before obtaining a change to F-1 status.

If you are transferring to your school from another school in the United States, you must complete a special school transfer procedure to maintain your F-1 status. This procedure must be completed within the first 15 days of starting classes. You must complete and submit the I-20 application and the required financial support evidence, and inform your previous school about the transfer so they can release the immigration record to the new university. If you plan to travel outside the United States before classes start, the university can send your transfer I-20 abroad.

Lastly, it is essential to review the specific requirements that the International Student Office may request and comply with them.

After Receiving the I-20 Form

Once you receive the I-20 form, there are several important steps you must follow to ensure your transition to the United States as an international student.

1. Review and Sign the I-20.

It is crucial to review the I-20 Form to ensure all the information is correct. If you find any errors, notify the International Services Office immediately. Sign and date the I-20 with blue ink at the bottom of the first page.

2. Pay the SEVIS I-901 Fee of $350.[3]

To pay online, visit fmjfee.com, complete the I-901 form online, and make the payment using a credit or debit card. Ensure that your name is written exactly as it appears on the I-20 Form, and include the SEVIS identification number and the university's school code. Print a copy of the online receipt and bring it with you to the visa appointment and when you travel to the United States.[4]

3. Apply for a Student Visa as Soon as Possible.

To apply, visit the travel.state.gov website to find the nearest U.S. consulate or embassy to your location. You must apply for the visa in your country of permanent residence and cannot do so more than 120 days before the start date indicated on your I-20. Application procedures, requirements, and processing times may vary, so it is important to contact the local U.S. embassy or consulate for specific instructions. This involves

---

[3] The specific fee amount may change at the State Department's discretion.
[4] More information can be found on the Department of Homeland Security (DHS) website: https://studyinthestates.dhs.gov/site/about-sevis

completing Form DS-160, which is the online application form for a non-immigrant visa. You must complete it and upload a photo of yourself according to specific requirements.

The Student Visa Interview

When preparing for the visa interview, it is crucial to be well-informed about the rules and ready to effectively answer the consular officer's questions. Here are some key aspects to consider.

By law, it is assumed that visa applicants plan to stay in the United States permanently. Therefore, it is essential to convince the consular officer that you will return to your home country upon completing your studies. Do not be discouraged if the officer is skeptical, as the primary reason for visa denial is failing to convince them of your intention to return to your country.

You must have a clear and valid academic goal in the United States. This includes demonstrating your qualifications and explaining how the studies will prepare you for a career in your country. Additionally, you need to present proof that you have sufficient financial resources to support yourself throughout the duration of the study program. Remember to be brief, honest, and direct in your answers.

When preparing for the interview, be ready to explain why you want to study in the United States, why you chose the study program and university, and how these studies will prepare you for a career in your home country. Present evidence of your academic qualifications and the original financial documents you provided to the university, ensuring they match exactly the information on the I-20 Form.

It is crucial to demonstrate that you have strong ties to your home country. This may include proof of permanent residence, such as a copy of the deed or lease agreement for your home. If your family owns a business, provide a letter from the bank describing it or copies of property deeds. If you have previously traveled to the United States as a visitor, emphasize that you returned to your country. A letter from a potential employer in your country stating they are interested in hiring individuals with the degree you will receive can also be helpful. Additionally, if you have siblings who studied in the United States and returned, provide a copy of their diploma and a statement from their employer.

Avoid emphasizing any connections you have with people or family members in the United States. Practice your English, as you are expected to be able to speak it and show your TOEFL score to the consular officer, unless your I-20 indicates that you will be studying English on campus. Do not mention working in the United States unless you have a teaching assistantship or scholarship. You must demonstrate that you can cover the costs of studying and living in the United States, as employment is strictly controlled by immigration and is not guaranteed.

If you began your studies under a different non-immigrant status and then changed to F-1, be prepared to explain how your original purpose in the United States changed to that of a full-time student. Provide copies of your transcripts to show your studies.

During the interview, you will know if your visa was approved or denied. If approved, you will be informed when the visa will be available in your passport. If denied, it is advisable to visit the International Students Office of your university for advice on how to strengthen your case.

Preparing for Your Arrival in the United States

To make your arrival in the United States as an F-1 student smoother, it is important to be well-informed about what to expect. You may be denied entry to the United States if you attempt to arrive more than 30 days before the start date of the academic program listed on your I-20 Form. You must carry certain documents with you when you arrive, and they should not be checked with your luggage. If your luggage is lost or delayed, you will not be able to present the documents at your port of entry, which could prevent you from entering the United States.[5] The necessary documents are:

1. A passport valid for at least six months after the program's end date.

2. F-1 visa (The consular officer may seal your immigration documents in an envelope and attach it to your passport).

3. I-20 Form.

4. Name and contact information of your "Designated School Official," including a 24-hour emergency contact number.

Additionally, it is recommended to carry:

- Proof of financial resources.

---

[5] For comprehensive information on entry processes, you can always refer to https://educationusa.state.gov/your-5-steps-us-study/prepare-your-departure.

- Evidence of your student status, such as recent tuition receipts and transcripts.
- A paper receipt of the SEVIS fee, Form I-797.

Upon Arrival at Your Port of Entry

Proceed directly to the passenger terminal area for arriving passengers. Have the following documents available: your passport, SEVIS Form (I-20), and the Customs Declaration Form (CF-6059). You will be asked to state your reason for entering the United States and provide information about your final destination. It is important to inform the U.S. Customs and Border Protection officer that you will be a student, along with the name and address of the university where you will enroll. Once the inspection is successfully completed, the inspecting officer will stamp your passport for the duration of status ("D/S") for F visa holders.

Arrival and Adaptation

Finally, upon arriving in the United States, ensure that you are prepared for your new life as a student. This includes familiarizing yourself with the environment, adapting to local customs, and ensuring compliance with all immigration regulations and academic requirements. The International Student and Scholar Services Office at your university will be an invaluable source of support and guidance during your stay in the United States.

Preparing to Live Away from Home

Living in a foreign country can be a cultural and emotional challenge. It is important to prepare for adapting to a new social and cultural environment. Familiarizing yourself with the customs, traditions, and social norms of your destination country will help you integrate more easily and avoid misunderstandings. Additionally, participating in extracurricular activities and student communities can enrich your experience and help you build a support network.

Do not neglect your physical and emotional well-being. Student life can be stressful, and being away from home can increase this stress. Finding a balance between your academic responsibilities and your personal well-being is vital. Make sure to know the health and wellness resources available at your university, and do not hesitate to seek help if needed.

Finding a support group, friends, and study companions within the university is essential to overcoming difficult moments while living away from home. Surrounding yourself with people who are going through similar experiences can offer not only emotional and social support but also practical help in the academic field. This support circle provides a sense of belonging and understanding, allowing you to face the challenges of cultural adaptation and the demands of the study program together. Additionally, having friends and study companions facilitates the exchange of ideas, resources, and strategies that enrich both learning and daily life.

Preparing comprehensively for this experience will allow you to achieve not only your academic goals but also personal and professional growth.

Immunization and Health Insurance

To successfully enroll in a university in the United States, it is essential for international students to complete all immunization and health insurance forms required by the institution.

The New York State Public Health Law, as a representative example of many jurisdictions in the United States, requires all students born on or after January 1, 1957, to be immunized against measles, mumps, and rubella. Students must present documentation proving they have received two doses of the measles vaccine and one dose of the mumps and rubella vaccines before classes begin. Without this proper documentation, attendance at classes will not be permitted. This requirement aims to protect public health and prevent outbreaks of contagious diseases in the university environment.

When enrolling in most universities, all F-1 and J-1 visa students are automatically enrolled in the institution's mandatory health insurance plan. This semester charge is included in the bill along with other university fees at the time of enrollment. Students with other immigration statuses also have the option to purchase this plan if they wish.

It is crucial for international students to carefully review the health insurance plan benefits, provider networks, and coverage conditions. Being well-informed about health insurance not only ensures compliance with university requirements but also provides peace of mind and security in case of medical emergencies. For more information on plan benefits, students can consult with their university's health services office.

3

LET'S TALK ABOUT MONEY

E ducational programs in the United States are often extremely expensive, especially for individuals from countries where the currency is not the U.S. dollar. Therefore, it is crucial to consider financing the program even before formally applying. Financial planning is an essential step to ensure that your educational experience abroad is manageable and successful.

As discussed previously, when applying for a student visa, one of your main concerns is demonstrating that you have the financial means to cover all costs associated with your studies and stay in the United States. Consular authorities require clear and convincing evidence that you can support yourself financially without the need to work illegally. This includes showing sufficient funds to cover tuition, accommodation, books, and other personal expenses.

Preparing a detailed financial plan that includes all available economic resources, such as personal savings, scholarships, loans, and family support is advisable. Additionally, you should be ready to present documents that support this information, such as bank statements, sponsorship letters, and any other financial evidence required by the embassy or consulate.

Comparison of Costs of Law Schools in the United States

Choosing a law school in the United States involves considering several factors, one of the most important being the cost. Below is a table comparing tuition fees and approximate living costs of some of the most prestigious law schools in the country. This information is crucial for international students who need to plan their budget and seek adequate financing for their studies.

University	Cost of Attendance (Approx.)	Duration	Location of Campus	Life Expenses (Approx.)
Harvard Law School	$77,100 per year	One year	Cambridge, MA	$29,100 per year
Yale Law School	$74,044 per year	One year	New Haven, CT	$22,800 per year
Stanford Law School	$74,475 per year	One year	Stanford, CA	$28,191 per year
Columbia Law School	$78,444 per year	One year	New York, NY	$25,797 per year
University of Chicago Law School	$76,479 per year	One year	Chicago, IL	$21,543 per year
New York University School of Law	$76,878 per year	One year	New York, NY	$26,800 per year
University of California, Berkeley Law	$73,000 per year	One year	Berkeley, CA	$26,014 per year
Georgetown University Law Center	$82,264 per year	One year	Washington, D.C.	$25,364 per year
University of Michigan Law School	$73,584 per year	One year	Ann Arbor, MI	$18,788 per year

The table above highlights the variability in tuition and living costs among different law schools in the United States. These costs can significantly influence your decision and financial planning. Besides tuition, students must consider the cost of living in the city where the university is located and the cost of books, which tend to be higher than in other countries. It is advisable to visit the official websites of the universities to obtain the most accurate and up-to-date information.[6]

Exploring Agreements Between Universities or Government Institutions

A viable option for financing your education in the United States is to investigate if there are agreements between your home university and U.S. universities. Many institutions have collaboration agreements that allow students to benefit from tuition discounts or exchange programs that significantly reduce costs. Additionally, some governments offer funding programs or scholarships for students wishing to study abroad. These programs are often designed to promote educational and cultural exchange and can provide sufficient funds to cover part or all of the educational costs.

Scholarships from Bar Associations

Bar associations, both in the United States and in your home country, can be an excellent source of funding. These organizations often offer scholarships specifically for law students who demonstrate high academic performance and a solid commitment to the legal profession. Scholarships from bar associations not only provide financial support but can also offer networking and professional development opportunities. It is important to research and apply for as many scholarships as possible to maximize your chances of receiving funds.

FAFSA and Student Loans

For U.S. residents and citizens, the **Free Application for Federal Student Aid (FAFSA)** is a fundamental tool for obtaining financial aid.

---

[6] Each university calculates its students ' approximate cost of living independently. The information in this table was taken from the various websites of the mentioned universities and varies each year, so it is important to always check the most updated version.

Through FAFSA, students can access a variety of federal aid, including student loans, grants, and work-study programs. While international students are not eligible for most federal aid, some may qualify for private or institutional loans offered by universities. It is crucial to explore all available options and understand the conditions of each loan, including interest rates and repayment terms.

Student Loans in Your Home Country

Another option for financing your education is to obtain student loans in your home country. Many financial institutions offer loans specifically designed for students planning to study abroad. These loans may have favorable terms and lower interest rates compared to private loans in the United States.

Before applying for a loan, it is essential to compare interest rates, fees, and other student-specific facilities. This comparison allows for informed financial decisions and finding the option that best suits individual needs, ensuring favorable conditions for post-study repayment in the United States. Additionally, consider how the exchange rate between your local currency and the U.S. dollar may affect payments.

Scholarships and Assistance Offered by the University

Many law schools in the United States offer scholarships, grants, and financial aid to help mitigate the cost of LL.M. programs. These funding opportunities may be based on merit, need, or a combination of both factors. It is crucial to research and inquire about the scholarships and financing options available at the universities of your interest. Some institutions also offer graduate assistant positions, which may involve research or teaching responsibilities in exchange for tuition waivers or stipends.

Merit-based scholarships are awarded based on outstanding academic, professional, or personal achievements. On the other hand, need-based scholarships are awarded based on the student's financial situation and ability to pay for educational costs.

Some universities offer **graduate assistantships** that include responsibilities such as research or teaching. These positions may provide a partial or total tuition waiver and, in some cases, a stipend to cover living expenses.

When applying for these aids, it is important to carefully review the eligibility criteria, application deadlines, and specific processes for each scholarship or assistantship. Early planning and submitting a well-documented and timely application are essential to maximize the opportunities for receiving funding.

International Opportunities

In addition to scholarships offered by universities, there are numerous external funding opportunities at the international level for LL.M. students. These can come from private foundations, government programs, or various cultural exchange organizations. Some of these include:

- **Fulbright Program:** This program offers scholarships for graduate studies in the United States and is available to students from numerous countries. Fulbright scholarships are highly competitive and seek to foster mutual understanding between the people of the United States and other countries.

- **Joint Japan/World Bank Graduate Scholarship Program:** This program offers financial support to students from developing countries who wish to study in graduate programs in various disciplines, including law, at U.S. universities.

- **Cultural Exchange Programs:** Various organizations promote cultural exchange programs that include funding for LL.M. studies. These programs aim not only to foster academic knowledge but also cultural understanding among students from different countries.

- **Private Foundations and Organizations:** Numerous private foundations and organizations offer scholarships for international students. These scholarships may be targeted at students from certain countries, specific areas of study, or those with particular characteristics and achievements.

When exploring these opportunities, it is essential to conduct thorough research and plan ahead. Each program and organization will have its own eligibility criteria and application deadlines. Submitting a complete and well-founded application can significantly increase the chances of receiving funding.

In summary, while the costs of studying an LL.M. in the United States can be high, there are multiple funding opportunities available both through universities and external sources. The key is proactive research and early planning to secure the financial support necessary for your education.

4

THINGS TO KNOW IN ADVANCE

By now, you have likely chosen the program that suits you best, considered how to manage your student visa and have a plan for financing your studies. However, before embarking on this exciting academic and professional journey, preparing adequately for the challenges and opportunities you will encounter is crucial.

Studying abroad, especially in an American institution, involves not only a change in the academic environment but also a shift in lifestyle. Adapting to a new culture, educational system, and social environment requires preparation and flexibility. From understanding academic and legal requirements to managing your finances and personal well-being, there are various aspects to consider to ensure a successful and enriching experience.

English for American Law School

If you have enrolled in an LL.M. program, the university will likely include or offer a legal English class, generally known as **"English for American Law School" (EALS)** or a similar term. The "English for American Law School" (EALS) program is a short course conducted before the start of the regular semester. It is specifically designed to help foreign-trained lawyers improve their understanding of the U.S. legal system and vocabulary before beginning their regular LL.M. studies. This course is also open to any professional wishing to enhance their legal English skills to gain an advantage in their career.

The primary goal of EALS is to provide students with the necessary tools to succeed in a U.S. legal environment. Students will learn from lawyers with extensive experience teaching non-native English speakers. The learning modules include:

- Fundamentals of the U.S. Legal System: Students receive a detailed introduction to the U.S. legal system, including its structure and functioning.

- Legal Writing and Argumentation: The focus is on legal writing and how to develop and present legal arguments effectively.

- Reading Legal Texts: Students learn to read and understand U.S. cases, statutes, and other legal texts.

These learning modules include lectures, discussions, writing assignments, and other exercises that will help students build the knowledge, skills, and confidence needed to:

Participating in an EALS program not only facilitates the academic transition to the U.S. legal system but also provides a solid foundation for professional success. Students develop a deep understanding of legal principles, improve their communication skills, and gain the confidence needed to interact effectively with colleagues and clients in a U.S. legal context.

In summary, the "English for American Law School" program is a valuable investment for any international lawyer wishing to pursue an LL.M. in the United States. It not only enhances linguistic and legal skills but also prepares students for the academic and professional demands of the U.S. legal environment.

U.S. Legal System

The U.S. legal system is complex and multifaceted, combining elements of Anglo-Saxon legal tradition with its own innovations. This system is based on the U.S. Constitution, which establishes the fundamental principles and framework of government and its relations with states and citizens. In addition to the Constitution, U.S. law comprises statutory laws, administrative regulations, and a vast body of case law derived from judicial decisions. A deep understanding of this system is crucial for any international lawyer wishing to study or practice in the United States, as it influences all aspects of law and legal practice in the country.

Common Law, Stare Decisis, and Rule of Law

A distinctive feature of the U.S. legal system is its tradition of **"common law."** Common law is a type of law derived from judicial decisions rather than written laws or statutes. Originally, U.S. courts created common law rules based on English common law. This continued until the U.S. legal system matured enough to develop its own common law rules, either from direct precedents or by analogy to similar areas of law already decided.[7]

In summary, common law is based on jurisprudence and previous judicial decisions. Judges use these past decisions as references to resolve current cases, ensuring consistency and continuity in the interpretation and application of the law. This allows the legal system to evolve and adapt to new circumstances without the need for formal legislative changes. Understanding this tradition of common law is essential for any international law student planning to study or practice in the U.S., as it significantly influences how laws are interpreted and applied in the country.

To understand common law and the value of precedent, one must know the doctrine of **stare decisis**. This principle is essential in the U.S. judicial system, establishing that courts must follow precedents set by previous judicial decisions. In Latin, stare decisis means "to stand by things decided." This means that when a court faces a case, it must base its decision on previous court rulings on similar issues. For a precedent to be binding, the previous court must have authority over the current court; otherwise, the precedent only has persuasive value.[8]

Stare decisis can operate both horizontally and vertically. Horizontal stare decisis occurs when a court follows its own precedents, such as when the Seventh Circuit Court of Appeals follows a previous decision of that same court. Vertical stare decisis applies when a court follows a precedent from a higher court, such as when the Seventh Circuit Court of Appeals follows a previous decision of the U.S. Supreme Court.

---

[7] Definition adapted from Cornell Legal Information Institute, available at https://www.law.cornell.edu/wex/common_law
[8] Definition adapted from Cornell Legal Information Institute, available at https://www.law.cornell.edu/wex/stare_decisis

This principle is fundamental for the stability and consistency of the legal system, ensuring that decisions are based on established rules and that similar cases are resolved uniformly over time.

All of the above would not be possible without the **rule of law**. This principle establishes that all individuals, institutions, and entities must be accountable under laws that are publicly promulgated, equally enforced, independently adjudicated, and consistent with international human rights principles. This concept ensures that no one is above the law and that everyone is treated with justice and respect.[9]

Courts play a crucial role in preserving the rule of law, as they are responsible for hearing and resolving the grievances of minorities and those with divergent opinions. By acting as guardians of justice, courts ensure that the fundamental rights of all individuals are protected and that the application of the law is consistent and fair. This fosters a legal system where transparency, equality, and respect for human rights are fundamental pillars.

These three concepts form the basis of the rest of the legal theories in the United States that we will review in this chapter and that you will learn in law school.

Constitution, Separation of Powers, and Historical Background

Understanding the formation of the U.S. Constitution is crucial to appreciating its current legal and political system. This process, which began with the early colonies and culminated in the creation of a strong federal government, is filled with significant events that laid the foundation for the nation.

The history of the United States begins with the arrival of the first European settlers. In 1607, the English founded Jamestown in Virginia, the first permanent settlement in North America. This initial period was marked by significant challenges, such as disease, conflicts with Indigenous peoples, and difficulties obtaining food. The Thirteen English Colonies on the East Coast gradually developed, each with its own economic and social structure.

---

[9] Definition adapted from United States Court, available at https://www.uscourts.gov/educational-resources/educational-activities/overview-rule-law

By the mid-18th century, the Thirteen Colonies began to prosper, but tensions with Great Britain also grew. The fiscal and commercial policies imposed by the British Parliament, such as the Navigation Acts and taxes without representation (e.g., the Stamp Act of 1765 and the Townshend Acts of 1767), generated deep discontent among the colonists.

On July 4, 1776, representatives of the colonies adopted the **Declaration of Independence**, primarily drafted by Thomas Jefferson. This declaration not only proclaimed separation from Great Britain but also established fundamental principles about individual rights and freedoms.

Securing the colonies' independence was not easy. The American Revolutionary War, lasting from 1775 to 1783, was an arduous and prolonged conflict. With support from France, Spain, and the Netherlands, colonial forces under the leadership of key figures such as George Washington eventually defeated British troops. The Treaty of Paris of 1783 formally recognized the independence of the United States.

After independence, the new United States faced the challenge of self-governance. In 1781, the **Articles of Confederation** were adopted, the first attempt to establish a national government. However, this system had significant weaknesses, such as the lack of power to levy taxes and regulate commerce, leading to ineffective management and interstate conflicts.

In 1787, a **Constitutional Convention** was convened in Philadelphia to address the deficiencies of the Articles of Confederation. The Convention brought together some of the most influential leaders of the time, including George Washington, James Madison, Benjamin Franklin, and Alexander Hamilton. After intense debates, the Convention produced a new document: the U.S. Constitution.

The Constitution established a federal government with a clear separation of powers between the executive, legislative, and judicial branches, and a system of checks and balances to prevent the abuse of power. Additionally, it introduced a system of federalism that balanced power between the national government and the states.

On September 17, 1787, the Constitution was signed by 39 of the 55 delegates. To take effect, it had to be ratified by at least nine of the thirteen states. This ratification process faced considerable opposition and debate, leading to the creation of two main factions: the Federalists, who supported the new Constitution, and the Anti-Federalists, who feared the centralization of power.

Ultimately, the promise to add a **Bill of Rights**, contained in the first ten amendments, guaranteeing the protection of fundamental individual liberties, helped secure ratification. On June 21, 1788, New Hampshire became the ninth state to ratify the Constitution, allowing its official implementation on March 4, 1789.

The adoption of the U.S. Constitution marked a decisive moment in the formation of the country. It established a governmental structure that has endured and evolved over time, providing a fundamental framework for governance and the rule of law in the United States. This early history of struggle and institutional building is crucial for understanding the context in which international lawyers may operate today in the U.S. legal system.

To fully comprehend the United States, it is essential to begin with its Constitution. Written over 200 years ago as the nation was forming from the 13 British colonies, this document serves as a master blueprint. Its seven sections (or Articles) outline the essential components of how the framers intended the government to function

Article I – The Legislative Branch: Article I establishes the Legislative Branch, whose main mission is to create laws. This branch is divided into two chambers: the House of Representatives and the Senate. Congress, the legislative body, has the power to draft and approve laws, borrow for the nation, declare war, and raise an army. Additionally, it has the ability to control and balance the other two federal branches, ensuring none becomes too powerful.

Article II – The Executive Branch: Article II describes the Executive Branch, which handles the daily operations of the government through various federal departments and agencies, such as the Department of the Treasury. At the head of this branch is the President of the United States, elected nationally. The president takes an oath to 'faithfully execute' the responsibilities as president and to 'preserve, protect, and defend the Constitution of the United States.' The president's powers include making treaties with other nations, appointing federal judges, department heads, and ambassadors, and determining the best way to direct the country and military operations.

Article III – The Judicial Branch: Article III defines the powers of the federal judicial system. It establishes that the highest court is the United States Supreme Court and that Congress has the power to determine the size and scope of lower courts. All judges are appointed for life unless they resign or are removed for misconduct. Those facing charges must be judged and evaluated by a jury of their peers, ensuring a fair judicial process.

Article IV – The States: Article IV defines the relationship between the states and the federal government. The federal government guarantees a republican form of government in each state, protects the nation and its people from foreign or domestic violence, and determines how new states can join the Union. Additionally, it suggests that all states are equal to each other and must respect the laws and judicial decisions of other states.

Article V – Amendments: Article V allows future generations to amend the Constitution if society requires it. Both the states and Congress have the power to initiate the amendment process, allowing the Constitution to evolve over time to meet new realities and needs.

Article VI – Debts, Supremacy, Oaths: Article VI establishes that the Constitution of the United States and all laws derived from it are the 'Supreme Law of the Land.' All officials, whether state legislators, members of Congress, the judiciary, or the executive, must take an oath to the Constitution, ensuring their loyalty and compliance.

Article VII – Ratification: Article VII details the procedures for ratification of the Constitution, including all individuals who signed the document, representing the 13 original states. This ratification process was crucial for the implementation and acceptance of the new framework of government throughout the country.

Following these articles are the amendments. The amendments to the United States Constitution are modifications or additions adopted to address issues not originally contemplated by the document's framers. Since its ratification in 1787, the Constitution has been amended 27 times. These amendments include the **Bill of Rights** (the first ten amendments), which guarantees fundamental freedoms such as freedom of speech and religion, and other amendments addressing important issues like the abolition of slavery, the definition of citizenship, and the right to vote, among others. The amendments reflect the Constitution's ability to adapt and evolve over time, ensuring it continues to protect the rights and needs of American citizens.

The **First Amendment** ensures that Congress shall make no law establishing an official religion or prohibiting the free exercise of religion. It also protects freedom of speech, press, assembly, and the right to petition the government for redress of grievances. This guarantees that citizens can express their opinions, practice any religion, and assemble peacefully without government interference.

The **Second Amendment** grants citizens the right to keep and bear arms. This right has been the subject of intense debate and discussion in American politics and jurisprudence, particularly concerning public safety and individual rights.

The **Third Amendment** prohibits the government from housing troops in private homes without the owner's consent. This amendment arose as a direct response to complaints during the American Revolution when colonists were forced to house British soldiers in their homes.

The **Fourth Amendment** protects citizens against unreasonable searches and seizures. The government cannot conduct searches without a warrant, and such warrants must be issued by a judge based on probable cause. This ensures citizens' privacy and security against arbitrary state interventions.

The **Fifth Amendment** establishes that citizens cannot be subjected to criminal prosecution and punishment without due process of law. It also protects against double jeopardy, ensuring that a person cannot be tried twice for the same offense. It includes protection against self-incrimination, allowing individuals the right to remain silent. The amendment also addresses the power of eminent domain, ensuring that private property is not taken for public use without just compensation.

The **Sixth Amendment** guarantees the right to a speedy and public trial by an impartial jury. It also ensures that the accused are informed of the charges against them, confront government witnesses, and obtain witnesses in their defense. Additionally, it grants the right to legal representation, ensuring all defendants have access to an attorney.

The **Seventh Amendment** preserves the right to a jury trial in civil cases. This guarantees that civil disputes, generally those involving monetary damages, can be decided by a group of citizens rather than just a judge.

The **Eighth Amendment** prohibits the imposition of excessive bail and fines, as well as cruel and unusual punishments. This amendment is crucial to ensuring that the justice system is fair and humane, avoiding disproportionate and abusive penalties.

The **Ninth Amendment** declares that the list of rights enumerated in the Constitution is not exhaustive and that the people retain all rights not listed. This means that citizens possess more rights than those explicitly specified in the Constitution.

The **Tenth Amendment** assigns all powers not delegated to the federal government, nor prohibited to the states, to the states or the people. This amendment underscores the principle of federalism, ensuring that states retain authority over all areas not specifically assigned to the federal government.

The Bill of Rights establishes fundamental rights for citizens and creates a legal framework to protect those rights from government interference, ensuring a just and equitable society.

Federalism

Another essential concept to understand the legal functioning of the United States is federalism. Federalism is a system of government in which the same territory is controlled by two levels of government. Typically, a national government governs broader territorial areas, while smaller subdivisions like states and cities handle local concerns. [10]

Both the national government and the smaller political subdivisions have the power to make laws and possess a certain level of autonomy from each other. This system of power distribution allows both the federal government and state governments to have legislative authority.

In the United States, the Constitution has established a system of "dual sovereignty," in which states have ceded many of their powers to the federal government but have also retained certain sovereignty. Examples of this dual sovereignty are described in the United States Constitution. As mentioned earlier, **Article VI** of the United States Constitution contains the Supremacy Clause. This means that when federal laws conflict with state laws, federal law prevails over state law.

Article I, Section 8 of the Constitution describes specific powers belonging to the federal government, known as enumerated powers. These powers include the ability to regulate interstate commerce, coin money, and maintain armed forces, among others. Meanwhile, the Tenth Amendment reserves powers to the states, as long as those powers are not delegated to the federal government. This includes creating school systems, overseeing state courts, creating public safety systems, managing businesses and commerce within the state, and administering local government.

---

[10] Definition adapted from Cornell Legal Information Institute, available at https://www.law.cornell.edu/wex/federalism

Federalism influences many aspects of studying and practicing law in the United States. For example, when studying Civil Procedure in the United States, it is crucial to remember that there is a federal judicial system and that each state has its judicial system. Therefore, the process of choosing a court requires lawyers and law students to analyze whether a case belongs in federal court, state court, or if the parties have the option to choose.

Federal and State Court Systems

In the United States, there is a diverse legal structure comprising more than 50 legal systems, as each of the 50 states, along with the federal government, has its own constitution, statutes, and courts.

The foundation of the federal judicial system is found in Article III of the United States Constitution, which establishes the Supreme Court as the highest judicial authority in the country. The Supreme Court, often referred to as the "court of last resort," has the highest appellate jurisdiction within the federal system. Article III also grants Congress the authority to create lower federal courts beneath the Supreme Court. These courts and judges are commonly referred to as Article III courts and judges.

Federal courts have limited jurisdiction, meaning they can only hear specific cases outlined in Article III, Section 2 of the United States Constitution and in Congressional statutes. This gives them jurisdiction over cases and controversies involving a federal question, involving parties from different states (diversity of citizenship), or arising between two states.

The federal courts are organized into several levels, including:

1. **United States District Courts:** These act as trial courts in the federal system. Each state has at least one federal judicial district, with some states having multiple districts.

2. **United States Courts of Appeals:** Also known as Circuit Courts, these courts handle appeals. There are 13 Circuit Courts. The first 11 circuits are geographically distributed. For example, the Court of Appeals for the Second Circuit covers Connecticut, New York, and Vermont, while the Ninth Circuit encompasses states like California, Arizona, and Washington. In addition to the mentioned courts, there are two additional appellate courts: the Court of Appeals for the District of Columbia Circuit and the Court of Appeals for the Federal Circuit, which has

jurisdiction over specialized cases such as government contracts and patents.

When a decision of a federal Circuit Court is appealed, the review is conducted by the Supreme Court of the United States, which can decide whether to accept an appeal from these courts, granting **certiorari** in a very limited number of cases. This system ensures that cases of national relevance are handled efficiently and uniformly, guaranteeing a coherent interpretation of federal laws across the country.

This chart below is useful for understanding the different courts in the federal system:[11]

Likewise, this map provides a geographic understanding of the different appellate circuits nationwide:[12]

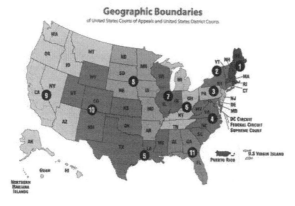

---

[11] Image property of the Judicial Learning Center, available at https://judiciallearningcenter.org/levels-of-the-federal-courts/
[12] Image property of the United States Courts website, available at https://www.uscourts.gov/about-federal-courts/federal-courts-public/court-website-links

On the other hand, state courts in the United States are organized similarly to federal courts, with a tiered structure that includes various levels of jurisdiction. Each state has its own judicial system, composed of:

1. Trial Courts: This is the basic level where cases are initially heard. The designation of these courts varies from state to state. For example, in Connecticut, they are called "superior courts," while in Florida, they are called "circuit courts."

2. Intermediate Appellate Courts: Many states have this intermediate level of review, where appeals from trial courts are handled. These courts ensure that cases are properly reviewed before reaching the state's highest court.

3. State Supreme Court: Each state has a highest-ranking court, usually called the "Supreme Court," although it does not always bear that name. This court is the final authority in interpreting the state constitution and laws, and its decisions are final within the state's jurisdiction.

State courts have general jurisdiction within the state's territory, meaning they can hear a wide range of cases, including those related to the state constitution and statutes.[13] In addition to general courts, many states have specialized courts to handle specific types of cases. For example, there are courts focused on low-value disputes, commonly known as "small claims courts." Some states also have courts for complex business matters, designed to handle high-complexity business disputes.

It is important to note that court names vary significantly from state to state. Although this can be confusing, the tiered structure of the judicial system remains consistent, with levels that allow for the orderly and systematic review and appeal of cases.

State court decisions, including those issued by state supreme courts, can be appealed to the United States Supreme Court under certain circumstances. This appeal is possible when a case involves federal questions, such as the interpretation of the United States Constitution or federal laws. If a party believes that a state decision violates constitutional rights or contradicts federal legislation, it can request that the United States Supreme Court review the case. However, the Supreme Court has discretion to accept or reject these appeals through a process known as granting certiorari. This mechanism ensures that only the most important

---

[13] Definition adapted from Cornell Legal Information Institute, available at https://www.law.cornell.edu/wex/state_court

constitutional or federal cases are reviewed, maintaining a balance between state sovereignty and federal government authority.

Legal Writing in the United States

Legal writing in the United States follows structured methods based on logical principles and established formats. A deep understanding of these methods is essential for succeeding in law school, professional exams like the bar exam, and daily legal practice. The foundation of this system lies in syllogism and the use of analogies and comparisons, applied in specific structures such as IRAC and its variations.

A syllogism is a form of deductive reasoning consisting of three parts:

1. Major Premise: This premise establishes a general legal rule or principle. For example, "All contracts not executed in good faith are void."

2. Minor Premise: Here, the specific facts of the case are applied to the general rule. For example, "The contract between A and B was executed with fraudulent intent."

3. Conclusion: Based on the previous premises, a logical conclusion is reached. For example, "Therefore, the contract between A and B is void."

Syllogism provides a clear and logical structure for legal analysis, helping lawyers formulate solid and coherent arguments. In addition to syllogism, analogies and comparisons are crucial tools in legal writing. These techniques allow lawyers to relate the case at hand to previous cases (precedents), helping to persuade the judge that a similar decision should apply. For example, if a court has previously decided that a certain type of behavior constitutes negligence, a lawyer can argue that similar behavior in the current case should also be considered negligent.

IRAC Method of Legal Writing

The most widely used method in the American legal community is IRAC, which stands for Issue, Rule, Analysis, and Conclusion.

- Issue: The first step in the IRAC methodology is to identify the legal issue being analyzed. This involves not only formulating a clear legal question but also incorporating some of the essential facts and parties of the case relevant to that question. Proper formulation of the issue is crucial as it frames the entire subsequent analysis. For example, in a negligence case, the issue might be: "Whether the defendant committed negligence by failing to provide adequate signage at the construction site?"

It is important to highlight both the parties involved and the specific facts of the case.

- Rule: The second part of IRAC involves stating the applicable legal rule. This section should include the law, relevant legal principles, and judicial precedents that apply to the identified issue. It is essential to be precise and thorough in this section, citing statutes, regulations, and previous cases that define the legal rule being applied. For example, in the context of a negligence case, this could include the standard of reasonable care established by case law and any specific statute that is relevant. The rule should be clearly articulated so that the reader can understand how it will be applied in the next section.

- Analysis: The analysis is the most extensive and detailed part of the IRAC methodology. Here, the legal rule is applied to the facts of the specific case. This section should show logical and systematic reasoning, demonstrating how the legal rule relates to the particular circumstances. It is essential to break down each element of the rule and compare it with the facts of the case, using analogies with previous cases when pertinent. For example, if the rule states that there must be a duty of care and a breach of that duty for negligence to exist, the analysis should examine whether, in this specific case, there was a duty of care and whether that duty was breached by the defendant's actions.

- Conclusion: The conclusion is the direct answer to the legal question posed in the Issue section, based on the analysis performed. This section should be clear and concise, summarizing the findings of the analysis and specifically answering the legal question. For example, in the negligence case, the conclusion might be: "Therefore, the defendant committed negligence by failing to provide adequate signage at the construction site, as there was a duty of care that was breached, resulting in foreseeable damages."

The IRAC format is highly structured, helping law students and professionals organize their thoughts and arguments clearly and logically. By following this method, it ensures that all relevant aspects of the case are addressed systematically. Additionally, the use of IRAC facilitates the objective evaluation of legal arguments, as each step of the reasoning is clearly delineated.

Advantages of Using IRAC

1. Clarity and Precision: IRAC forces lawyers to be precise and clear in their analysis, ensuring that important details are not overlooked.

2. Structured Organization: The logical structure of IRAC facilitates the presentation of arguments coherently and orderly.

3. Consistency: The consistent use of IRAC helps standardize legal writing, making legal documents easier to follow and understand.

4. Effective Communication: IRAC enhances the communication of complex ideas, allowing lawyers to articulate their arguments persuasively and comprehensibly.

Variations of IRAC

There are several variations of IRAC, each adapted for different legal contexts, but all maintain the basic structure of legal analysis. Some of the most common variations include:

- **CREAC:** Conclusion, Rule, Explanation, Application, Conclusion. This structure begins and ends with the conclusion, emphasizing the answer to the legal issue from the start.

- **IREAC:** Issue, Rule, Explanation, Application, Conclusion. Similar to IRAC, but adds a detailed explanation of the rule before the analysis.

- **CRAC:** Conclusion, Rule, Analysis, Conclusion. Emphasizes the initial and final conclusions, with a direct focus on the rule and analysis.

A deep understanding of these systems is essential for academic and professional success in the legal field in the United States. In law school, these structures are fundamental for completing assignments, writing essays, and tackling exams. In professional practice, they are indispensable for drafting clear and persuasive legal documents and presenting strong arguments in court. Mastering syllogism, analogies, comparisons, and formats like IRAC and its variations allows lawyers to structure their thinking and communicate their ideas effectively, which is crucial for their performance in the American legal system.

Example of Text Written with IRAC

This IRAC example stands out for its clarity and organization, making it an effective model for analyzing legal issues. It begins by clearly identifying the legal issue and then establishes a rule based on the applicable laws. The analysis examines how these legal principles apply to the specific facts of the case, providing a deep understanding of the situation. Finally, the conclusion offers a direct and well-supported answer to the initial issue, demonstrating how legal reasoning can lead to a coherent and well-founded resolution.

Issue:

The issue is whether the parties are citizens of different states and the amount in controversy exceeds $75,000 as to meet the requirements for diversity jurisdiction.

Comment: When formulating the issue, it is crucial to incorporate parts of the rule and specific facts of the case to clearly and precisely pose the question. This helps focus the analysis on the central point of the controversy.

Rule:

Federal courts have limited jurisdiction and can only hear specific cases. The United States Code, 28 USC, establishes the circumstances under which a lawsuit can be filed in a federal district court, including cases of federal question and diversity jurisdiction. Specifically, diversity jurisdiction requires that any plaintiff in the case must be a citizen of a different state than any defendant, and that the amount in controversy exceeds $75,000. Regarding domicile, physical presence in the state and the intent to remain there indefinitely are considered. The relevant domicile is the one existing at the time the lawsuit is filed. Concerning the amount in controversy, a single plaintiff may aggregate all necessary claims against the same defendant to exceed the $75,000 requirement.

Comment: When writing the rule, organize the information from general to specific, like an inverted triangle. Start with the general jurisdiction and move towards the specific details of the case and applicable rules.

Analysis:

In this case, the lawsuit was filed in a federal district court, so there must be jurisdiction based on a federal question or diversity of citizenship. Clearly, no federal question is involved since both the contract and tort claim arise under state law. Therefore, it is necessary to analyze whether the diversity requirements are met. At the time of filing the lawsuit, the Buyer, as the plaintiff, had already moved to State Y and decided to establish permanent residence there, forming his citizenship in State Y. At the same time, the Seller was still a citizen of State X because he did not move to State Y until a week after the lawsuit was filed. Additionally, regarding the amount in controversy, although the contract claim is only for $2,500, the plaintiff may aggregate as many claims as desired against the same defendant, so the total amount here is $502,500, thus satisfying the amount in controversy requirement as well.

Comment: In the analysis, each sentence should reflect a sentence from the rule applied to the specific facts of the case. This helps demonstrate how the conclusion is reached through the logical application of the rule to the particular circumstances.

Conclusion:

Therefore, the court should not dismiss the tort or contract claims, as there is subject matter jurisdiction based on diversity of citizenship.

Comment: The conclusion should directly answer the initial issue. It is essential for it to be clear and direct, providing a resolution based on the previous analysis.

In general, it is advisable to separate each section, although not necessarily naming them. The presented IRAC example provides practical guidance on how to apply this method to real cases. By breaking down each component and offering detailed recommendations for its development, it demonstrates how to structure an effective legal analysis. Practicing with examples like this helps students master the technique, enabling them to tackle legal problems with greater confidence and precision. IRAC not only organizes legal thinking but also reinforces the ability to argue logically and convincingly, essential skills both academically and professionally.

Do you think you are ready to apply it?

Put IRAC Structure into Practice

Facts:

An electronics store called "TechWorld" published an advertisement in the newspaper that said: "This Saturday at 10 a.m., the first 5 customers will receive a new, state-of-the-art smartphone for only $5.00. No prior reservations accepted." Mr. Rodríguez arrived at the store at 9:30 a.m. and was one of the first 5 customers in line. However, when he tried to buy the smartphone, the store manager told him that the offer was only for customers who had previously purchased a product at TechWorld in the past year. Mr. Rodríguez had never shopped at TechWorld before, so they did not sell him the smartphone. Mr. Rodríguez decided to sue TechWorld for breach of contract.

Can Mr. Rodríguez win a lawsuit to compel TechWorld to honor the terms of the advertisement?

Rule of Law:

In the case of Lefkowitz v. Great Minneapolis Surplus Store, Inc., the court decided that an advertisement can constitute an offer if it is clear, definite, and leaves nothing to negotiation, so that a reasonable recipient can conclude that an offer has been made. Once accepted, a valid contract is formed. Restrictions not mentioned in the original offer cannot be applied subsequently.

Instructions:

Use the IRAC method to analyze this fact pattern.

1. Issue: Identify the legal issue being analyzed.

2. Rule: Describe the general rule provided.

3. Analysis: Apply the rule to the facts of the case.

4. Conclusion: Reach a conclusion based on your analysis.

Did You Know?

The real case of **Lefkowitz v. Minneapolis Surplus Store** occurred in 1957 and centers on a dispute over the sale of a fur coat. In summary, Lefkowitz saw an advertisement in the newspaper offering top-quality fur coats, valued at $100, for just $1. Lefkowitz was one of the first to arrive at the store, but he was denied the sale of the coat due to a store policy that limited the offer to women only. Lefkowitz sued the store, arguing that he had accepted the advertised offer and that the store had breached the contract by refusing to sell him the coat.

The Minnesota Supreme Court held that the advertisement was a unilateral offer and that Lefkowitz had accepted the offer by showing up at the store. The court determined that the store's policy limiting the offer to women was invalid and that Lefkowitz had the right to purchase the coat at the advertised price.

If you feel motivated to write an IRAC essay on the given example, go ahead! You can send it to my email at laramaike25@gmail.com for feedback and comments on your analysis. I am here to help you with whatever you need.

Reading Legal Texts

Lawyers must deal with a wide variety of texts, including cases, memoranda, motions, contracts, statutes, and regulations, among others.

However, one of the most important elements for understanding legal discourse in the United States is judicial cases. Familiarizing oneself with the structure and components of cases is essential for effective reading and proper legal analysis.

To approach reading legal texts effectively, it is useful to first do a quick read to get a general idea of the main points and organization of the case. This approach allows you to quickly identify the structure and key points before a more detailed reading. Underlining, highlighting, or circling important words and phrases helps to highlight essential elements of the text. Additionally, having a dictionary on hand can be helpful for understanding unfamiliar legal terms. Writing brief notes in the margins can facilitate quick reference and help summarize ideas, ask questions, or highlight important points during the reading.

Elements of a Case

Caption: The case caption includes essential information such as the names of the parties involved and the identification of the case. This component is fundamental to contextualizing the case and understanding who is involved in the legal dispute. Knowing who the parties are provides a basis for understanding the dynamics and relationships that led to the litigation.

Case Citation: The case citation provides the specific legal reference for the case, indicating where it can be found in the judicial reports. This is crucial for verification and consultation of the case details in the legal context. An accurate citation allows lawyers and law students to quickly locate the case and review its full details in the relevant legal records.

Case citations are essential for legal research and writing, allowing precise referencing of previous judicial decisions. Each part of a case citation provides specific information that helps locate the case. Here is a breakdown of the typical sections found in a case citation:[14]

---

[14] Image property of the Richmond Law Library, available at https://law-richmond.libguides.com/c.php?g=129583&p=846335

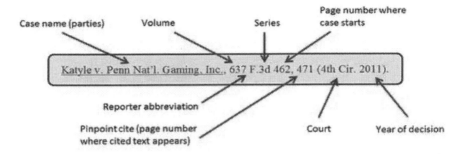

The name of the case includes the names of the parties involved in the case. The plaintiff's name is generally listed first, followed by the defendant's name. The volume number indicates the volume of the reporter in which the case is published. Reporters are collections of judicial decisions, and each volume contains multiple cases. The reporter abbreviation identifies the specific series of reporters that publishes the case. Common abbreviations include "U.S." for United States Reports and "F.2d" for Federal Reporter, Second Series. The first page of the case indicates the page on which the case begins in the reporter volume. The court and year section specifies the court that decided the case and the year of the decision.

Author of the Opinion: Knowing the author of the opinion can offer perspective on the approach and interpretation of the law, as different judges may have varied approaches to similar legal issues. The style and judicial philosophy of the author can significantly influence the writing and conclusions of the case, providing additional context for legal analysis.

Facts: The facts of the case narrate the story and events that led to the legal dispute, describing the actions and events that brought about the lawsuit between the parties. This section describes the problem or dispute that occurred before the lawsuit was filed, placing the sequence of events on a timeline preceding the filing date. The facts are usually found at the beginning of the case, use the past tense, and do not contain legal citations, providing a clear and chronological narrative of the relevant events.

Procedural History: The procedural history describes the legal decisions of the lower courts and details the legal arguments presented before, during, and after the trial. This section narrates the actions and events that occurred when and after the lawsuit was filed, explaining how the case progressed through the judicial system. It often uses the past tense and mentions terms like trial court, appeal, motions, and interim orders. The procedural history usually appears at the beginning of the case.

Issue: The issue of the case establishes the legal questions the court must resolve. This section uses the present or past tense and is generally formulated as a question. It uses phrases like "the issue is whether." Issues can be procedural, substantive, or both, and are fundamental to understanding the court's focus in the case.

Rule / Rule of Law: The rule or rule of law explains the law that the court is applying, including legal citations. Sources of law can be statutes, judicial decisions, state or federal constitutions, or administrative regulations. This section may cite treatises and other secondary sources and frequently uses the present tense. The statements are usually general and not specific to the facts of the case.

Analysis / Discussion / Reasoning: The analysis applies existing rules of case law to the facts of the case, comparing the case to similar previous cases. It provides reasons that support the decisions and explains the court's logic behind its ruling. Other courts' decisions are often discussed, using the past tense. This section may contain legal citations and make comparisons, analogies, or suggestions of hypothetical situations.

Holding: The holding of the case provides the court's answer to the issues raised and resolves the problems of the case. It uses both the present and past tenses and common phrases like "we hold that..." or "we conclude that...". This section contains specific information about the case and clearly states the court's decision.

Disposition: The disposition of the case indicates the specific action the court takes to resolve the case. It uses keywords like "affirmed," "reversed," or "remanded" and generally appears at the end of the case. The disposition is crucial to understanding the final outcome of the case and the legal implications of the court's decision.

Mastering these reading strategies and understanding the components of a case is vital for any law student or legal professional. The ability to analyze and synthesize legal information effectively not only enhances comprehension of the subject but is also crucial for the daily practice of law.

How does a case look?

Below, you will see a classic case to practice identifying the different sections of a judicial case. This case, **James L. O'Keefe v. Lee Calan Imports, Inc. v. Field Enterprises, Inc.**, involves a dispute over an advertisement and an alleged contract for the sale of a car at an incorrect price. As you read the case, try to identify the key sections we have discussed: the facts, the issue, the rule, the analysis, and the conclusion. This exercise will help you become familiar with the structure of a case and improve your ability to effectively create a case brief.

James L. O'Keefe v. Lee Calan Imports, Inc. v. Field Enterprises, Inc.
128 Ill. App. 2d 410 (Appellate Court of Illinois, First District, Third Division 1970)

Opinion

McNAMARA, Justice.

Christopher D. O'Brien brought suit against defendant for an alleged breach of contract. O'Brien died subsequent to the filing of the lawsuit, and the administrator of his estate was substituted in his stead. Field Enterprises, Inc., was joined as a third party defendant, but was dismissed from the suit, and that order of dismissal is not involved in this appeal. Plaintiff and defendant filed cross-motions for summary judgment. The court denied plaintiff's motion for summary judgment and granted defendant's motion. This appeal follows. The facts as set forth in the pleadings and cross-motions for summary judgment are not in dispute.

On July 31, 1966, defendant advertised a 1964 Volvo Station Wagon for sale in the Chicago Sun-Times. Defendant had instructed the newspaper to advertise the price of the automobile at $1,795. However, through an error of the newspaper and without fault on part of defendant, the newspaper inserted a price of $1,095 for said automobile in the advertisement. O'Brien visited defendant's place of business, examined the automobile and stated that he wished to purchase it for $1,095. One of defendant's salesmen at first agreed, but then refused to sell the car for the erroneous price listed in the advertisement.

Plaintiff appeals, contending that the advertisement constituted an offer on the part of defendant, which O'Brien duly accepted and thus the parties formed a binding contract. Plaintiff further contends that the advertisement constituted a memorandum in writing which satisfied the requirements of the Statute of Frauds.

It is elementary that in order to form a contract there must be an offer and an acceptance. A contract requires the mutual assent of the parties. Calo, Inc. v. AMF Pinspotters, Inc., 31 Ill.App.2d 2, 176 N.E.2d 1 (1961).

The precise issue of whether a newspaper advertisement constitutes an offer which can be accepted to form a contract or whether such an advertisement is merely an invitation to make an offer, has not been determined by the Illinois courts. Most jurisdictions which have dealt with the issue have considered such an advertisement as a mere invitation to make an offer, unless the circumstances indicate otherwise. 157 A.L.R. 744 (1945).

As was stated in Corbin on Contracts § 25 (1963): 'It is quite possible to make a definite and operative offer to buy or to sell goods by advertisement, in a newspaper, by a handbill, or on a placard in a store window. It is not customary to do this, however; and the presumption is the other way. Neither the advertiser nor the reader of his notice understands that the latter is empowered to close the deal without further expression by the former. Such advertisements are understood to be mere requests to consider and examine and negotiate; and no one can reasonably regard them otherwise unless the circumstances are exceptional and the words used are very plain and clear.'

In Craft v. Elder & Johnston Co., 38 N.E.2d 416 (Ohio App.1941), defendant advertised in a local newspaper that a sewing machine was for sale at a stated price. Plaintiff visited the store, attempted to purchase the sewing machine at that price, but defendant refused. In holding that the newspaper advertisement did not constitute a binding offer, the court held that an ordinary newspaper advertisement was merely an offer to negotiate. In Ehrlich v. Willis Music Co., 93 Ohio App. 246, 113 N.E.2d 252 (1952), defendant advertised in a newspaper that a television set was for sale at a mistaken price. The actual price was ten times the advertised price. The court found that no offer had been made, but rather an invitation to patronize defendant's store. The court also held that defendant should have known that the price was a mistake. In Lovett v. Frederick Loeser & Co., 124 Misc. 81, 207 N.Y.S. 753 (1924), a newspaper advertisement offering radios for sale at 25% To 50% Reductions was held to be an invitation to make an offer. Accord, People v. Gimbel Bros., 202 Misc. 229, 115 N.Y.S.2d 857 (1952).

We find that in the absence of special circumstances, a newspaper advertisement which contains an erroneous purchase price through no fault of the defendant advertiser and which contains no other terms, is not [an] offer which can be accepted so as to form a contract. We hold that such an advertisement amounts only to an invitation to make an offer. It seems apparent to us in the instant case, that there was no meeting of the minds nor the required mutual assent by the two parties to a precise proposition. There was no reference to several material matters relating to the purchase of an automobile, such as equipment to be furnished or warranties to be offered by defendant. Indeed the terms were so incomplete and so indefinite that they could not be regarded as a valid offer.

In Lefkowitz v. Great Minneapolis Surplus Store, 251 Minn. 188, 86 N.W.2d 689 (1957) defendant advertised a fur stole worth $139.50 for sale at a price of $1.00, but refused to sell it to plaintiff. In affirming the judgment for plaintiff, the court found that the advertisement constituted a valid offer and, upon acceptance by plaintiff, a binding contract. However in that case, unlike the instant case, there was no error in the advertisement, but rather, defendant deliberately used misleading advertising. And in Lefkowitz, the court held that whether an advertisement was an offer or an invitation to make an offer depended upon the intention of the parties and the surrounding circumstances.

In Johnson v. Capital City Ford Company, 85 So.2d 75 (La.App.1955), defendant advertised that anyone who purchased a 1954 automobile could exchange it for a 1955 model at no additional cost. Plaintiff purchased a 1954 automobile and subsequently attempted to exchange it for a 1955 model, but was refused by defendant. The court held that the advertisement was an offer, the acceptance of which created a contract. However, in that case, the advertisement required the performance of an act by plaintiff, and in purchasing the 1954 automobile, plaintiff performed that act. In the case at bar, the advertisement did not call for any performance by plaintiff, and we conclude that it did not amount to an offer.

Because of our view of these proceedings, it is unnecessary to consider the issue of whether the newspaper advertisement constituted a memorandum in writing satisfying the requirements of the Statute of Frauds.

The judgment of the Circuit Court is affirmed.

Judgment affirmed.

DEMPSEY, P.J., AND SCHWARTZ, J., concur.

You have already seen the structure of a case in the example of James L. O'Keefe v. Lee Calan Imports, Inc. Were you able to identify the different sections? Recognizing and understanding these parts is essential to mastering the reading and analysis of legal texts. In the next section, we will see how to create a "case brief" based on this case, which will further help you consolidate your skills and better prepare for your law studies.

Case Briefs

In law school in the United States, a fundamental part of learning involves reading and analyzing judicial cases. Students must tackle dozens of cases each week in various subjects, which can make it difficult to remember all the details. An effective strategy for managing this reading load is to create case briefs. A case brief is a concise summary of a judicial case that extracts and organizes the most important information. This document allows students to have the key points of each case at hand, facilitating review and study.

In American legal culture, the ability to summarize and paraphrase is highly valued. It is essential to be able to express the same information in a shorter and clearer way. This is especially important in the Facts section of a case brief, but it also applies to the sections of Issue, Decision, and Analysis. However, there are terms and phrases with specific legal meanings that must be used as they are, without substituting them with your own words. Finding the right balance between paraphrasing and using precise terminology requires practice and experience.

Although there is no single correct way to write a case brief, as these documents are primarily intended for the personal use of the student, there are some common elements that are usually included. The quality of a case brief depends on its usefulness in preparing the student for class and on what the professor considers important.

The elements of a case brief are the same as those found in a full judicial case: Facts, Procedural History, Issue, Rule or Legal Standard, Analysis or Discussion, Decision, and Disposition. These components allow students to synthesize the crucial information of the case, facilitating their understanding and study.

Writing a case brief is a skill that improves with practice. There is no absolutely right or wrong way to do it, as each professor may have different expectations about what is important in a case. The best way to improve is to try, compare with classmates' summaries, and adjust according to the professor's focus in class. Additionally, many students add notes to their case briefs during class based on what the professor discusses or questions, which helps refine and deepen their understanding of the case.

What does a case brief look like?

Previously, you read the case of James O'Keefe v. Lee Calan Imports, Inc. v. Field Enterprises Inc. and made an effort to identify the different sections of the case. Now, we will show you what a case brief of this same case would look like. Note how the facts, procedural history, issue, rule, analysis, decision, and disposition are summarized and organized. This example will help you visualize how to break down a case clearly and concisely, facilitating your understanding and study of legal material.

JAMES O'KEEFE v. LEE CALAN IMPORTS, INC. v. FIELD ENTERPRISES INC.
128 Ill. App. 2d 410 (Appellate Court of Illinois, First District, Third Division 1970)

Facts

- On July 31, 1966, the defendant advertised the sale of a 1964 Volvo Station Wagon.
- The defendant instructed the newspaper to price the car at $1,795, but the newspaper made an error and published a price of $1,095.
- O'Brien visited the defendant, wished to buy the car for $1,095, but the defendant refused to sell it at that price.

Procedural History

- O'Brien sued the defendant for an alleged breach of contract, then O'Brien died, and the estate administrator was substituted.
- Field Enterprises was joined as a third party but was dismissed from the case.
- The court denied the plaintiff's motion for summary judgment and granted the defendant's motion for summary judgment.

- The plaintiff contends that the acceptance constitutes a binding contract and that the advertisement is a written memorandum satisfying the Statute of Frauds requirements.

Issue

- Whether a newspaper advertisement is an offer that can be accepted to form a contract or merely an invitation to make an offer.

Rule

- An advertisement is an invitation to make an offer unless it uses clear and specific words or requires the performance of an act.
- Offer + Acceptance = Contract.

Analysis

- There was no consensus or mutual assent between the two parties.
- There was no reference to material matters relating to the purchase that the defendant should have offered.
- The incomplete and vague terms could not be considered an offer

Holding

- The advertisement is considered only an invitation to make an offer. Without special circumstances, newspaper ads with errors and no other terms do not constitute an offer to form a contract.

Disposition

- Affirmed.

This chapter has covered crucial areas for your success in the American educational environment. From the need to master "English for American Law School" to understanding the fundamentals of the legal system and the IRAC methodology for legal writing, we have addressed essential tools for your academic development. Additionally, we have explored strategies for critical reading of cases, which are fundamental to understanding and analyzing jurisprudence. By preparing for this challenging academic environment, you will be equipped to actively participate in class and conduct solid and well-founded legal research.

Taking advantage of available resources, such as libraries, workshops, and tutoring, is also essential for excelling in your study program. These resources will provide you with additional support to strengthen your language, writing, and critical thinking skills. By investing time and effort in developing these skills, you will be better prepared to face academic challenges and stand out in your studies and your future legal career.

5

ETHICS FOR LAW STUDENTS

In the United States, as in most countries, lawyers are subject to mandatory codes of ethics that are fundamental to the practice of the profession. These codes regulate the professional conduct of lawyers and ensure they act with integrity, competence, and respect towards the judicial system and their clients. The responsibility for approving and enforcing these codes of ethics falls on the judiciary of each state, meaning each state may have specific variations in its ethical rules.

In addition to state codes, there are the **American Bar Association 's (ABA) Model Rules of Professional Conduct**. Although they do not have the force of law, the ABA's Model Rules serve as a comprehensive guide and are often adopted or adapted by states when formulating their own codes of ethics. These rules set standards on competence, confidentiality, conflicts of interest, client communication, and other critical areas of professional conduct for lawyers.

In this chapter, we will explore the most relevant ethical principles for law students and future lawyers, and how these principles apply both in law school and in professional practice. Understanding these codes of ethics from the beginning of your legal education will prepare you to act responsibly and professionally in your career.

Ethics in the legal profession is not only a regulatory obligation but also an essential pillar for maintaining public trust in the judicial system. Lawyers have the responsibility to serve justice and represent their clients with honesty and diligence. The codes of ethics ensure that lawyers behave fairly and equitably, avoiding conduct that could harm their clients, the administration of justice, or the reputation of the profession. From the first day in law school, it is important for students to internalize these ethical principles and apply them in their studies and practices. Ethics is not only learned in theory but also practiced in everyday life.

In this regard, it is important to keep in mind **Rule 8.1 of the ABA Model Rules of Professional Conduct**. This rule, titled "Maintaining the Integrity of the Profession," sets forth the ethical obligations of applicants for admission to the bar and lawyers concerning applications for admission or disciplinary matters.

Rule 8.1 of the ABA Model Rules of Professional Conduct: Maintaining the Integrity of the Profession

An applicant for admission to the bar, or a lawyer in connection with a bar admission application or in a disciplinary matter, shall not knowingly make a false statement of material fact; or fail to disclose a fact necessary to correct a known misunderstanding in the matter, or fail to respond to a lawful demand for information from an admissions or disciplinary authority, except that this rule does not require disclosure of information otherwise protected by Rule 1.6.

Commentary on Rule 8.1

The duty imposed by this rule extends to both individuals seeking admission to the bar and lawyers. Therefore, if a person makes a material false statement in connection with an admission application, this can be the basis for subsequent disciplinary action if the person is admitted, and in any event, it may be relevant in a subsequent admission application. The duty imposed by this rule applies to both the lawyer's own admission or discipline and that of others. Therefore, it is a separate professional offense for a lawyer to make a misrepresentation or intentional omission in connection with a disciplinary investigation of the lawyer's own conduct. Paragraph (b) of this rule also requires correction of any prior false statement in the matter and affirmative clarification of any misunderstanding by the admissions or disciplinary authority that the person involved becomes aware of.

Implications of Rule 8.1

Rule 8.1 underscores the importance of honesty and transparency in the bar admission process and disciplinary proceedings. This rule imposes specific obligations on applicants and lawyers to ensure that the information provided to admissions or disciplinary authorities is complete and truthful. Besides avoiding false statements, applicants and lawyers must correct any known misunderstanding and respond to legitimate requests for information from the authorities. Failing to disclose can be as harmful as making a false statement. The rule states that false statements or failure to disclose can be the basis for future disciplinary actions, even if the person is initially admitted. This highlights the importance of integrity at all stages of a legal career.

In summary, Rule 8.1 of the ABA Model Rules of Professional Conduct emphasizes the ethical obligation of lawyers and applicants to act with integrity and transparency. Complying with this rule is essential to maintaining trust in the legal profession and ensuring that lawyers are worthy of the responsibility that comes with practicing law.

Examples of Ethical Violations

Before embarking on legal practice, it is crucial for law students to understand and adhere to the ethical principles that govern our profession. In this section, we will explore concrete examples of ethical violations that may arise in the academic environment of law school. These examples illustrate situations in which students may face difficult decisions that test their integrity and commitment to established ethical standards. By examining these cases, we aim to foster deep reflection on the importance of honesty, transparency, and responsibility in forming ethically responsible and competent lawyers.

- Misrepresentation of facts: Misrepresentation of information to professors, administration, or potential employers constitutes a significant ethical violation. This includes any false statement about personal achievements or misleading information about others to gain unfair advantages in the academic or professional realm.

- **Plagiarism:** Plagiarizing, whether in written work or other assignments, is a severe ethical violation that undermines the fundamental principles of learning and research. Failure to properly attribute original sources constitutes a violation of academic and professional integrity.

- **Improper use of academic materials:** Any improper or unauthorized manipulation of academic resources, such as exams or copyrighted materials, constitutes an ethical violation. Respecting established regulations is essential to maintaining fairness and integrity within the educational environment.

- **Subversion of attendance policies:** Falsifying attendance records, such as signing in for an absent classmate, constitutes a violation of law school attendance policies. Accuracy in documenting attendance is crucial for assessing academic progress and maintaining integrity in the educational environment.

- **Subversion of examination policies:** Any action intended to violate established rules for the administration and conduct of academic exams constitutes an ethical violation. This includes unauthorized use of electronic devices during exams or unauthorized communication between students.

- **Failure to disclose a violation:** Failing to report a known ethical or academic violation constitutes an additional ethical infraction. Transparency and responsibility are fundamental to maintaining integrity in the educational and professional community, promoting a culture of honesty and compliance with ethical standards.

By exploring these examples of ethical violations in the law school environment, we emphasize the importance of adhering to established ethical principles and standards. Students should reflect on how these situations may influence their professional development and commit to acting with integrity in all their academic interactions and future legal practices. By respecting these standards, they not only strengthen their own ethical reputation but also contribute positively to the integrity and prestige of the legal system as a whole.

Possible Consequences in Law School

Failure to meet the established ethical and academic standards in law school can result in various consequences, ranging from disciplinary measures to long-term repercussions in one's professional career. The following are some of the possible consequences at the discretion of the law school:

- Failing grade on an assignment: A negative evaluation on a task or exam as a direct result of an ethical or academic violation.

- Disciplinary action and grievance procedures: Initiation of formal disciplinary actions and grievance processes according to the policies established by the educational institution.

- Suspension or expulsion: The possibility of being temporarily suspended or expelled from law school as a consequence of serious or repeated infractions.

- Referral to the Dean, Vice Dean of Academics, or Dean of Students: Referral of the case to higher administrative authorities for review and appropriate disciplinary action.

- Damage to reputation: Loss of trust and credibility within the academic and professional community, affecting personal and professional reputation.

- **Notations on the academic record:** Official record of the infraction in the student's academic file, which may influence future academic and professional opportunities.

- **Professional discipline in practice:** Potential impact on the professional career, including the possibility of facing ethical or disciplinary sanctions once in active practice of the legal profession.

- Future disclosure requirement: Requirement to disclose the ethical or academic infraction in future job applications, bar admission, or other professional entities.

These consequences underscore the importance of maintaining high standards of ethical and academic conduct during law school. It is essential for students to understand and respect established regulations, not only to meet educational requirements but also to cultivate a reputation of integrity and professional responsibility that will last throughout their careers.

Character and Fitness for Bar Admission

When submitting an application for bar admission, one of the crucial components evaluated is the character and fitness of the applicant. This process, known as **"Character and Fitness,"** is essential to ensure that only those individuals demonstrating integrity and responsibility are admitted to practice law. Below, the importance of maintaining ethical rules is explained, along with how violations can complicate this process.

The character and fitness evaluation process is a preventive measure used by bar admission committees to ensure that future lawyers possess the moral qualities and ethical conduct necessary to practice law. Lawyers must not only possess legal knowledge but also demonstrate behavior reflecting honesty, reliability, and respect for the law. This scrutiny is vital because lawyers have a fiduciary responsibility to their clients and play a crucial role in the administration of justice.

Maintaining ethical rules during law school and in personal life is essential to avoid future complications when applying for the bar. The bar admission committee reviews the applicant's personal, academic, and professional history. Any ethical or academic violation, such as falsifying information, plagiarism, or misconduct, can be a warning sign that questions the applicant's fitness. Transparency and honesty are crucial, as any attempt to conceal an ethical violation may result in automatic disqualification or future disciplinary proceedings.

An attorney's reputation begins to form from the moment they enter law school. Actions and decisions made during this period can have a lasting impact on the perception of colleagues, professors, and future employers. Maintaining ethical and responsible conduct helps build a solid and trustworthy reputation, essential for legal practice. Ethical violations can have significant long-term repercussions, including the need to disclose them in all future professional applications, the possibility of facing disciplinary sanctions, and irreparable damage to personal and professional reputation.

Maintaining ethical behavior and adhering to established standards is not only crucial to meet law school requirements but also fundamental to ensure a positive evaluation during the bar admission process. A history of integrity and responsibility not only facilitates admission but also lays the foundation for a successful and respected career in legal practice.

In conclusion, we must emphasize that ethics are a fundamental pillar in the education and practice of any lawyer. It is crucial to remember that ethical violations during law school can have serious consequences, from academic sanctions to potential disqualification in the bar admission process. Rule 8.1 of the ABA Model Rules of Professional Conduct underscores the importance of maintaining integrity, demanding honesty and transparency in both bar admission and any disciplinary matter.

Furthermore, it is necessary to understand the gravity of the consequences that may arise from unethical behavior, including reputation loss and future professional complications. Lastly, we addressed the importance of the character and fitness evaluation process, highlighting how a history of integrity and ethical conduct is vital to being admitted to the practice of law.

In summary, adherence to ethical principles is essential for academic and professional success, and crucial for maintaining public trust in the legal system. By incorporating these principles into their daily and professional lives, law students prepare for a successful career and contribute to preserving justice and integrity in the legal profession.

6

A TYPICAL DAY IN CLASS

We have covered everything from preparing to live away from home to the crucial ethical aspects to consider as a law student. Now, let's delve into what your day-to-day in law school will look like. Understanding the daily routine and knowing what to expect will help you navigate the challenges and opportunities that lie ahead.

The Importance of the Syllabus

As soon as the semester begins, the enrolled courses will post the syllabus on the platform. The syllabus is a vital document provided by each professor at the start of the semester. This detailed document includes the course description, learning objectives, class schedule, required readings, exam dates, assignment deadlines, and course policies.

Reviewing the syllabus is crucial because it allows you to plan and organize your time effectively, ensuring you are aware of all course expectations and requirements. Additionally, the syllabus provides a clear overview of the course structure and helps you anticipate the weekly workload, enabling you to distribute your study and preparation time evenly.

The syllabus also serves as a contract between the professor and students. By carefully reading it, you can better understand what is expected of you in terms of participation, attendance, and the quality of work. This includes details on how your assignments and exams will be evaluated, as well as class policies regarding attendance and punctuality. Knowing these policies helps you avoid misunderstandings and maintain a good relationship with your professors.

Furthermore, the syllabus may include information about additional resources the professor may offer, such as office hours, review sessions, and supplemental study materials. Taking advantage of these resources can be key to your success in the class. It's also a good idea to periodically review the syllabus throughout the semester to ensure you are meeting all requirements and important deadlines.

In addition to the syllabus, it is essential to familiarize yourself with the university's general policies regarding exam make-up, absences, and other administrative procedures. These policies, often detailed in the student handbook or on the university's website, complement and supplement the content of each course syllabus. Understanding these regulations allows you to better grasp your rights and responsibilities as a student, and the consequences of not complying with established norms.

For instance, university policies on exam make-up can vary significantly from specific course policies. Knowing the procedures and requirements in advance for requesting a make-up due to illness or emergency allows you to act quickly and appropriately if an unforeseen situation arises. Similarly, being aware of rules regarding justified and unjustified absences helps you avoid issues that may affect your academic performance and grades.

University general policies may also include information on academic and disciplinary conduct, the use of university facilities and resources, and the process for filing complaints or appeals. Being well-informed about these aspects allows you to navigate the academic environment with greater confidence and security, preparing you to address any situation that may arise during your time in law school.

In summary, familiarizing yourself with both the syllabus of each course and the university's general policies provides you with a comprehensive understanding of academic and administrative expectations. This dual information is essential for maintaining a successful academic trajectory and avoiding misunderstandings or issues that could affect your university experience.

Keeping Up with Readings

Staying current with the weekly assigned readings listed in the syllabus is crucial. These readings, which often consist of court cases, form the basis of class discussions and learning in law school. Reading and understanding each case is fundamental to your academic and professional success. To achieve this, it is recommended to create "case briefs" for each case you read. A case brief is a concise summary that highlights relevant facts, the legal issue, the applicable rule, analysis, and the case's conclusion. This exercise will not only help you digest the material better but also prepare you for questions and discussions in class.

Understanding cases involves more than just reading them; you must analyze and reflect on them. Look for other related cases that may help you better understand the context and implications of judicial decisions. This approach allows you to see how the law applies in different circumstances and helps you develop critical and analytical thinking skills. Additionally, formulating hypothetical questions about the cases prepares you for potential questions the professor may ask in class. These questions often explore variations in facts and how these variations can affect the application of the law. Practicing with these questions will make you feel more confident and prepared to participate in class discussions actively.

Moreover, discussing cases and readings with your classmates can be beneficial. Forming study groups is an excellent way to exchange ideas, clarify doubts, and delve deeper into topics. The diversity of perspectives will enrich your understanding and help you better grasp the nuances of each case.

Keeping up with readings and deepening your analysis of cases will provide you with a solid foundation of knowledge and skills that are essential for your academic performance and future career as a lawyer. This discipline will help you stay prepared and make the most out of every class and discussion.

Socratic Method and Cold Calls

Legal education relies heavily on the Socratic method, a pedagogical technique dating back to ancient Greece used to foster critical thinking and deep understanding of legal concepts. This method is characterized by a question-and-answer approach where the professor challenges students to think analytically and articulate their thoughts clearly and logically. The primary goal is to help students develop essential skills for

- 65 -

legal practice, such as analytical reasoning, logical reasoning, and effective articulation of arguments. This technique not only enhances understanding of legal topics but also promotes intellectual independence and confidence in reasoning and argumentation abilities.

In a Socratic method-based class, the professor does not directly impart information but guides students through a series of strategic questions. These questions are designed to help students discover answers for themselves and gain a better understanding of the underlying principles of the subject being studied. This approach requires students to come to class well-prepared, having read and analyzed the assigned material. Learning is largely the responsibility of the student, who must be willing to actively participate in discussion and embrace the intellectual challenge this method entails. Students must be proactive in their preparation, analyzing cases in detail and anticipating possible questions the professor may pose.

Preparing for a Socratic class involves reading the assigned cases and deeply analyzing them. Students should be able to identify relevant facts, legal issues, applicable rules, and court reasoning. Furthermore, they should be prepared to discuss how those principles may apply to different facts or how they might change if circumstances were different. This level of preparation ensures that students can participate meaningfully in the discussion and fully benefit from the Socratic method. The ability to analyze a case from multiple perspectives and anticipate potential variations in facts is crucial for success in these classes.

One of the key tools of the Socratic method is the **"cold call."** Cold calls involve the professor randomly calling on students during class to answer questions about the cases studied. These questions can range from case facts and applicable legal rules to analysis and implications of the judicial decision. The idea behind cold calls is to ensure that all students remain engaged and prepared, as anyone could be called upon to participate at any moment. This technique fosters a culture of constant preparation and attention in class, as not knowing when you will be asked to speak requires you to always be ready. Additionally, the pressure of cold calls can simulate the pressure of real-life situations in legal practice, better preparing students for their future careers.

For example, the professor might ask: "What are the relevant facts of this case?", "What is the legal rule applied here?", or "How would you justify the court's decision?". These questions not only compel students to know the material but also help them develop skills to think and respond quickly under pressure, an essential competency for any lawyer. Regular practice in responding to these questions in class prepares students for similar situations in their future careers, where they will need to think and react quickly and accurately. Moreover, by facing and overcoming the challenge of cold calls, students develop the confidence necessary to argue and defend their positions effectively.

In addition to cold calls, the Socratic method includes the use of **"Socratic questions."** These are questions designed to deepen student analysis and take the discussion to a deeper level. For example, the professor might ask: "What would have happened if the facts of the case had been different?", "How would this rule affect a case with different circumstances?" or "What are the possible criticisms of this judicial decision?". These questions are designed to explore the limits and implications of legal rules, as well as to foster critical and analytical thinking. This type of questioning requires students not only to understand the case in question but also to be able to apply it to new situations and to think creatively about how legal rules may evolve or be interpreted in different ways.

The Socratic method also encourages discussion and debate among students. During a class, it is common for the professor to allow students to respond to or challenge their classmates' answers, creating a dynamic and collaborative environment. This interaction not only enhances students' understanding but also helps them develop important skills for legal practice, such as the ability to listen and respond effectively to others' arguments. Classroom debate allows students to see multiple perspectives on the same issue, improving their ability to construct and deconstruct arguments effectively.

Furthermore, the Socratic method prepares students for the demands of real legal practice, where lawyers must be prepared to think quickly, articulate their arguments persuasively, and respond to unexpected questions and challenges from judges, opponents, and clients. The ability to adapt and respond effectively in these situations is crucial to success in legal practice.

In summary, the Socratic method and cold calls are fundamental in legal education. Arriving prepared to class is crucial for success in law school and prepares students for the rigorous and demanding world of legal practice. The ability to think quickly, articulate clear arguments, and respond to difficult questions are skills developed and perfected through this method, preparing future lawyers for the challenges they will face in their professional careers. The dedication and effort invested in preparing for Socratic classes translate into a solid legal education that equips students with the tools necessary to excel in their profession.

Taking Notes During Classes

Taking notes effectively during class is a crucial skill for success in law school. The complexity of the material and the fast pace of class discussions make it essential to capture as much information as possible. Below are some strategies and considerations for taking notes efficiently and organized.

It is important to take extensive notes during classes. Socratic discussions and detailed explanations by professors often contain valuable information not found in assigned texts. Taking extensive notes allows you to review and better understand the material later, especially when preparing for exams.

Some professors may have specific policies regarding the use of electronic devices in class. Some prefer students to take notes by hand to avoid distractions and enhance information retention. Studies have shown that taking notes by hand can improve understanding and memory, as it requires deeper processing of information. If your professors require handwritten notes, make sure you have all necessary materials like notebooks and pens, and be prepared for this note-taking method.

Using Abbreviations

Using abbreviations can speed up the note-taking process and help you capture more information in less time. Here are some common abbreviations used in law school that will be useful: [15]

- ∏ or P: Plaintiff
- Δ or D: Defendant
- §: Section
- K: Contract or contracts
- Jdx: Jurisdiction
- Rev'd: Reversed
- Aff'd: Affirmed
- TC: Trial court

---

[15] Abbreviations provided by Berkeley Law, available at https://www.law.berkeley.edu/files/abbreviations.doc.

- AC: Appellate court
- DC: District court
- SC or S.Ct.: Supreme court
- TRO: Temporary restraining order
- MTD: Motion to dismiss
- Ev.: Evidence
- b/c: Because
- a/st: Against
- E'er: Employer
- E'ee: Employee
- w/: With
- w/o: Without
- re:: About
- Inxn: Injunction
- Summ. Jdg. or S.J.: Summary judgment
- FRCP: Federal rules of civil procedure
- R, R2: Restatement of Law, Restatement Second

Using these abbreviations will allow you to take faster notes and keep up with the pace of the class.

Cornell Method of Note-Taking

The Cornell method is a structured technique for note-taking that can be particularly useful in law school. This method divides the page into three sections: notes column, key words column, and summary. Here's how to use it:

1. Notes Column: Use the widest section of the page to write your notes during class. This is where you'll capture main information, case discussions, arguments, and Socratic questions.

2. Key Words Column: To the left of the notes column, reserve a narrower section for key words and questions. After class, review your notes and jot down key words, important concepts, and questions that may arise. This will help you quickly identify important points when reviewing your notes later.

3. Summary: At the bottom of the page, write a brief summary of the notes. This step is beneficial because it forces you to review and reflect on the material, cementing acquired knowledge. Reviewing and summarizing your notes helps consolidate information into long-term memory and identify any areas needing clarification or further study.

Other Note-Taking Methods

In addition to the Cornell method, there are other approaches that may be helpful depending on your learning style and the specific demands of your classes:

1. Mind Mapping Method: This method uses visual diagrams to hierarchically organize information and show relationships between concepts. It's particularly useful for complex and visual topics, helping you see the structure of information at a glance.

2. Outline Note-Taking Method: Organize notes into hierarchical levels, with titles and subtitles representing main information and details. This method is effective for structuring your notes logically and clearly, facilitating review and study.

3. Charting Note-Taking Method: Divide the page into columns and rows, creating a table to organize information. This method is useful for comparing and contrasting different concepts, cases, or arguments.

By exploring and adapting different note-taking methods, you can find the one that best suits your needs and maximize your understanding and retention of the material.

Again, effective note-taking is an essential skill in law school. By combining adequate preparation, the use of abbreviations, and techniques such as the Cornell method or mind mapping, you can significantly improve your ability to capture and organize information during classes. Consistent practice and adjusting your note-taking methods according to the specific needs of each class and professor will help you maximize your learning and academic performance.

After Classes

Once classes are over, another crucial phase of your learning begins: reviewing and organizing your notes. This process is essential for consolidating what you've learned and preparing for success in final exams. Reviewing your notes after each class is fundamental. Dedicate time each day to read your notes and ensure you understand all concepts. If something is confusing or unclear, this is the perfect time to clarify it. You can consult your textbooks, search for additional resources online, or ask your classmates or professors for more information.

Translating ideas into clearer terms is an important step in understanding the material. Rewrite or rearrange your notes if necessary, using your own words to explain concepts. This not only improves your understanding but also facilitates future review. Additionally, organize your notes logically, grouping related topics and making connections between different concepts.

As topics are concluded, it's good practice to start creating an outline of the material. Outlining involves structuring your notes and readings into a more condensed and organized format. These outlines will serve as study guides and effective summaries for final exams. In the next chapter, we will explore in detail how to create and use these effective outlines.

Participating in study groups can be extremely beneficial. Discussing the material with your peers allows you to see different perspectives and clarify doubts. Moreover, explaining concepts to others is an excellent way to reinforce your own understanding. Ensure the group stays focused and structured to make the most of study time.

Do not hesitate to use additional resources to complement your studies. There are numerous law exam preparation books, educational videos online, and learning platforms that can provide you with additional explanations and examples. Taking advantage of these resources can help you better understand challenging topics and prepare more comprehensively for exams.

The work doesn't end when classes are over. Reviewing and organizing your notes, along with creating outlines and participating in study groups, are essential activities to ensure your success in law school. As you prepare for final exams, these practices will help you consolidate your knowledge and approach the material more effectively. In the next chapter, we will explore in detail how to create effective outlines that will prepare you for final exams.

Although it may seem overwhelming to do everything required in law school, it's crucial to remember to take care of your mental health. Use study and organization methods that have worked for you in your academic life so far, and don't hesitate to seek support when needed. Maintain a balance between your academic responsibilities and personal well-being to ensure sustainable success and an enriching experience.

7

EXAMS IN LAW SCHOOL

E xams in law school are a fundamental part of the academic process and play a crucial role in evaluating students' performance. Unlike other fields of study, law exams not only assess students' knowledge but also their ability to apply legal principles to complex situations and their skill in critical thinking under pressure.

This chapter is designed to guide you through everything you need to know to successfully tackle exams in law school, from preparation and study techniques to specific strategies for each type of exam. You will learn how to structure essay responses, approach multiple-choice questions, and effectively analyze cases. Additionally, we provide tips for managing your time and handling stress during exam season. By mastering these skills, you will improve your academic performance and prepare yourself for the professional challenges you will face as a lawyer.

Understanding the Exam

One of the crucial first steps in preparing for law school exams is thoroughly understanding the exam format and its specific requirements. This includes several key aspects that can influence your study approach and how you prepare for exam day.

First, it is essential to determine whether the exam will be open book or closed book. An **open-book** exam allows the use of reference materials such as textbooks, notes, and statutes during the exam. This can be advantageous for consulting specific details of the law or directly citing relevant cases. On the other hand, a **closed-book** exam does not permit the use of additional materials during the test, requiring rigorous preparation and a deep understanding of the material that must be memorized.

Additionally, it is important to identify whether the exam will consist of multiple-choice questions or essays. In the case of **multiple-choice questions**, they typically begin with a fact pattern or scenario of facts that serves as the basis for the subsequent questioning. This questioning presents different options that students must analyze and select as their answer. On the other hand, **essay** exams require students to develop detailed and reasoned responses to a specific legal question based on a provided fact pattern.

Regardless of the type of exam, the **fact pattern** plays a crucial role. This set of facts presents a complex legal situation that students must analyze and correctly apply to relevant legal rules. Understanding the details and nuances of the fact pattern is essential for crafting persuasive and accurate legal arguments. This skill enhances exam performance and reflects real legal practice, where clarity and precision in identifying relevant facts are crucial for successful case outcomes and legal defense.

In legal exams, it is crucial to distinguish between distractors or **"red herrings,"** which are irrelevant facts that may divert attention from central legal issues, and legally relevant facts. Distractors can lead to time wastage and unnecessarily complicate the response, whereas identifying and focusing on legally relevant facts is crucial for crafting precise and persuasive legal arguments. This skill not only enhances exam performance but also reflects real legal practice, where clarity and precision in identifying relevant facts are fundamental for successful case outcomes and legal defense.

Other considerations include the percentage that the exam represents in your final course grade and any specific policies the professor may have regarding the exam structure. Some exams may include a combination of multiple-choice questions and essays, requiring versatile preparation tailored to multiple question formats.

Once you have fully understood the exam format and requirements, you can implement effective strategies for your preparation:

- **Practice with past exams:** Using past exams or practice tests provides a valuable opportunity to familiarize yourself with the specific exam format and professor expectations. The law school library often offers access to an archive of past exams, organized by course and professor, allowing you to practice under conditions similar to exam day. This helps you identify areas of strength and areas needing more attention, as well as adjust your study strategy accordingly.

- **Develop outlines and summaries:** Creating detailed outlines and summaries of key topics is an effective technique for organizing and consolidating information. By synthesizing complex concepts into a clear and concise format, you can visualize the course structure and ensure you deeply understand each topic. These resources are especially useful for a quick review before the exam and refresh your memory on specific points.

- **Participate in study groups:** Joining study groups provides an opportunity to discuss legal issues and theories with your peers. Through these discussions, you can not only reinforce your understanding of the topics but also see different perspectives and approaches to addressing legal problems. Explaining concepts to others and hearing different interpretations can help you solidify your own understanding and resolve any doubts you may have.

- **Effective time management:** Practicing time management during your studies and exams is essential for maximizing your performance. Organize your study time effectively by allocating specific periods to review each topic and practice exam exercises. During the actual exam, keep an eye on the clock to ensure you complete all sections within the allotted time, prioritizing questions that may carry more weight in the final grade.

- **Care for mental and physical health:** Maintaining a healthy balance between study and rest is crucial for optimal performance during the exam period. Ensure you take regular breaks and get sufficient sleep to maintain your energy and concentration. Practice stress management techniques, such as meditation or exercise, to maintain a positive mindset and reduce anxiety before and during exams. Taking care of your physical and emotional well-being will help you maintain high academic performance in the long run.

Fully understanding the exam and adapting your preparation accordingly will provide you with the confidence and skills necessary to successfully tackle academic challenges in law school.

Tips for Each Type of Exam

Multiple-Choice Exams

1. Read the question: Begin by carefully reading the question or initial inquiries of the exam. This will give you a clear idea of the themes and legal concepts that will be evaluated.

2. Analyze the fact pattern: After understanding the question, proceed to analyze the fact pattern or provided scenario of facts. Identify key details and legal situations that will be relevant for answering the questions.

3. Review answer options: Once you have a clear understanding of the question and fact pattern, review the available answer options. Evaluate each one in relation to the presented facts and applicable legal rules. Eliminate incorrect options to improve your chances of selecting the correct answer.

The following is a real example of how a multiple-choice exam question with a fact pattern might appear:

"A woman from State A filed an action against a retailer in a state court in State B. The lawsuit alleged that the retailer had not delivered $100,000 worth of goods for which the woman had paid.

Twenty days after being notified, the retailer, which is incorporated in State C and has its principal place of business in State B, filed a notice of removal in a federal district court in State B.

Was the action properly removed?

(A) No, because the notice of removal was not timely filed.

(B) No, because the retailer is a citizen of State B.

(C) Yes, because the parties are citizens of different states and there is more than $75,000 in controversy.

(D) Yes, because the retailer is a citizen of both State B and State C."[16]

Essay Exams

1. Understand the question: Start by fully understanding the essay question or provided inquiry. Identify the specific legal issues that must be addressed in your response.

---

[16] Copyright © 2016, 2021 by the National Conference of Bar Examiners. All rights reserved.

2. Analyze the fact pattern: After understanding the question, thoroughly analyze the fact pattern or scenario of facts. Highlight key elements and legal relationships that must be discussed in your response.

3. Apply the IRAC method: Organize your response using the IRAC method (Issue, Rule, Application, Conclusion).

4. Use relevant cases and doctrines: Support your arguments using relevant legal cases and doctrines. This will demonstrate your deep understanding of the material and strengthen your response.

5. Review and refine: Review your response upon completion to ensure you have covered all aspects of the question. Adjust any necessary details to improve the clarity and coherence of your argumentation.

Adopting these steps will help you effectively prepare for both types of exams, optimizing your ability to demonstrate your knowledge and skills during the evaluation period.

The following is an example of a typical essay for a law school exam:

"In the city of Albany, New York, three friends, Emily, David, and Lisa, decide to establish a general partnership called Albany Artisan Crafts, dedicated to selling local crafts and organizing creative workshops. According to their partnership agreement, all purchases over $500 must be pre-approved by at least two partners.

However, Lisa, without obtaining the required approval, signs two contracts on behalf of Albany Artisan Crafts: she purchases $100 worth of watercolors from a local store, $1500 worth of fabrics for painting, and acquires a ring for $3000. In each contract, she is identified as 'Albany Artisan Crafts, by Lisa Thompson, Partner.'

Two months later, the materials supplier presents Albany Artisan Crafts with an invoice for $4600 for the outstanding materials. Emily, one of the partners, refuses to pay the invoice, arguing that Lisa did not have authorization to make these purchases.

1. Is Albany Artisan Crafts liable on the contracts for the purchase of (a) the watercolors; (b) the fabrics; and (c) the ring?

2. What if, before Lisa made these purchases, David sends the supplier a copy of the partnership agreement by certified mail, return receipt requested, signed by himself? What would be the result?"

This essay example provides a robust platform for legal analysis due to its complexity and the various situations posed. By exploring the decisions of Albany Artisan Crafts partners and the legal implications of their actions without proper authorization, this case offers multiple perspectives and areas of discussion. This scenario not only challenges students' understanding of legal rules but also fosters the development of critical skills for legal argumentation and application of the law in complex business contexts.

Preparation through Outlining

Preparing an effective outline is essential for organizing your studies systematically and comprehensibly before exams. This method allows you to visualize the course structure, identify key concepts, and prioritize the most relevant information. Here is a detailed process for creating a solid outline and practical tips to optimize its use.

The outline acts as a detailed roadmap that facilitates understanding and memorization of the material. By dividing the content into clear and logical sections, it helps establish connections between different concepts and topics of the course. This helps you study more efficiently and prepares you to effectively respond to exam questions that may address diverse and complex topics. Creating an effective outline requires attention to detail and clarity in organization. Here are some practical tips to maximize the usefulness of your outline:

- **Simplify and Clarify:** Use clear and concise language in your outline. Avoid redundancy and ensure each point is easily understandable. Use legal and technical terms precisely and appropriately to accurately reflect legal and juridical concepts.

- **Visual Organization:** Use visual techniques such as bullet points, numbering, or hierarchies to structure your outline clearly and organized. This will facilitate review and allow you to quickly identify key information during your studies and exams.

- **Include Examples and Cases:** Integrate practical examples and relevant cases into your outline. These examples will help illustrate theoretical concepts and apply them to practical situations, thereby strengthening your understanding and memory of the material.

- **Continuous Update:** Regularly review and update your outline as you progress in your studies and acquire new knowledge. Ensure it accurately reflects your current understanding and areas requiring more attention or additional study.

- **Practice with Your Outline:** Use your outline as an active tool during your study. Use it to make summaries, review, and solve practical problems. This will help consolidate the information and prepare effectively for exams.

Steps to Create an Outline

1. Identify the Main Idea: Start by clearly defining the main topic or subject you want to cover in your outline. This starting point will help you establish the overall framework of your study and outline the specific objectives you want to achieve.

2. Breakdown of Subtopics: Divide the main idea into more specific and relevant subtopics. Each subtopic should capture an important aspect of the course and serve as a focal point for your study. This breakdown will allow you to address each topic in more detail and precision.

3. Details and Subdivisions: For each subtopic, add additional details and subdivisions. Include key concepts, relevant theories, notable cases, and specific examples that help consolidate your understanding. This hierarchical structure will allow you to understand the relationship between different elements of the course and strengthen your ability to analyze and synthesize legal information.

4. Tiered Organization: Organize your outline in a tiered manner, from the most general ideas to the most specific. This will allow you to visualize the hierarchy of information and understand how concepts within the course are interrelated. Tiered organization will also facilitate review and recap, as you can quickly identify the main topics and key details.

Using the outline effectively not only improves your exam preparation but also strengthens your overall understanding of the law by organizing and structuring information coherently and accessibly. By providing you with a clear and detailed guide, the outline helps you efficiently manage the vast amount of legal information you need to master for academic and professional success.

Example of an Outline

This example of an outline focuses on Personal Jurisdiction, showing how to effectively structure information for a clear and detailed understanding. The outline follows an organized hierarchy, starting with general ideas and breaking down into more specific points. It uses bullet points and numbers to clearly delineate the different levels of information, making it easier to identify the main topics and subtopics. This method of structuring is ideal for law students as it helps visualize the relationship between broad concepts and specific details, ensuring that all important aspects of the topic are addressed logically and coherently.

A. Personal Jurisdiction

I. Basic Idea

    a. Refers to the court's power over the parties. The court always has personal jurisdiction over the plaintiff; the question is about the defendant. Personal jurisdiction belongs to the parties and they have the power to waive it.

    b. **General Personal Jurisdiction:** The forum is where the defendant is domiciled or served with process, and can be sued for a claim that arose anywhere.

        1. The domicile of a **natural person** is where they physically live and intend to remain.

        2. The domicile of a **corporation** is where it is incorporated and its Principal Place of Business (PPB).

        3. A **partnership** is domiciled at the domicile of any of its partners.

    a. **Specific Personal Jurisdiction:** The claim arises from the defendant's contacts with the forum.

II. Two-Step Analysis:

    a. **Comply with a State Long-Arm Statute:** Generally extends to the full extent of the constitution.

    b. **Comply with the Due Process Clause of the Constitution:** Requires the defendant to have such minimum contacts with the forum that jurisdiction does not offend traditional notions of fair play and substantial justice (International Shoe).

    1. **Contact:** There must be a relevant contact between the defendant and the forum state:

        i. **Purposeful Availment:** The contact must result from a voluntary act of the defendant. Even causing an effect in the forum satisfies the test.

        ii. **Foreseeability:** It must be foreseeable that the defendant could be sued in the forum according to a reasonable person's standard.

    1. 2. **Relatedness:** The plaintiff's claim must arise from the defendant's contact with the forum.

    2. **Fairness:** Whether the jurisdiction would be fair under the circumstances.

i.   If it puts the defendant at a severe disadvantage in litigation. Economic hardship alone is insufficient.

ii.   State's interest.

iii. Plaintiff's interest.

Exam Day

Exam day is crucial and can be a stressful experience, but with good preparation and some practical tips, you can handle it effectively. Here are some key points to keep in mind.

First, try to arrive early at the exam location. Plan your route in advance and account for traffic or any unforeseen delays that could make you late. Arriving early not only gives you enough time to find the correct room but also allows you to acclimate to the environment, find a comfortable seat, and ensure you have everything you need for the exam. This anticipation helps reduce anxiety and allows you to start the exam with a calm and focused mindset.

The exam is usually completely anonymous. Instead of your name, you will be assigned an anonymous identification number that you must place on your exam. This system ensures impartiality in grading, as graders will not know to whom each exam belongs. Make sure you understand how to use this number and place it correctly on your exam to avoid any administrative issues that could affect your grade. Familiarize yourself with this procedure before exam day to ensure there are no surprises.

The exam will be administered by a proctor, a person who has no direct relation to your law school. This proctor is responsible for reading the exam instructions and keeping track of time. Listen carefully to the instructions provided by the proctor and make sure you understand them completely before starting. If you have any questions, this is the appropriate time to ask. Additionally, the proctor ensures that the environment is suitable and free of distractions, which is essential for your concentration.

Stay calm and focus on managing your time well during the exam. Use the first few minutes to review the entire exam and plan how you will tackle each section. This will help you stay organized and ensure you do not leave any questions unanswered. Divide your time evenly among the questions and make sure to leave a few minutes at the end to review your answers. This extra time can be crucial for correcting errors or completing answers you initially left incomplete.

Bring with you all permitted materials you might need, such as extra pens, pencils, and any other allowed items according to the exam instructions. Some exams allow the use of certain resources like legal codes or reference books. Make sure you know in advance what materials are permitted and prepare them in an orderly manner so you can access them easily during the exam.

Finally, remember that exam day is an opportunity to demonstrate everything you have learned. Maintain a positive attitude and trust in your preparation. The key is not to let stress dominate you. Relaxation techniques such as deep breathing or small mental breaks can help you stay calm and focused. With these tips in mind, you will be well-equipped to face the exam effectively and with confidence.

It is also important to take care of your physical and mental health in the days leading up to the exam. Ensure you get enough sleep the night before, eat well, and stay hydrated. Avoid excessive consumption of caffeine or any other substances that might alter your mood or concentration. A well-cared-for body and mind are crucial for optimal performance.

Post-Exam: Evaluation and Results

After completing your exam, the evaluation process and post-exam procedures are handled meticulously to ensure fairness and academic integrity. Here are some key points to consider:

Everything related to the exam is managed by the **Registrar's office**. This office is responsible for coordinating the logistics of the exam, from its administration to its final evaluation. For multiple-choice exams, the Registrar's office handles grading using answer templates provided by the professor. This method ensures an objective and accurate evaluation, eliminating any potential bias in grading.

For essay exams, the process is a bit more complex to maintain impartiality. After exams are submitted, the Registrar collects all essay files and assigns them an anonymous identification number, removing any information that could identify the student. These anonymous files are then sent to the responsible professors for evaluation. Professors review and grade each essay without knowing the author's identity, ensuring that grades are based solely on the content and quality of the submitted work.

Anonymity in the evaluation process is crucial to ensure all students are judged fairly. By grading essays without knowing to whom they belong, professors can focus on the structure, legal analysis, clarity, and accuracy of each response without external influences. This system promotes a fair academic environment and helps maintain the integrity of the evaluation process.

Once exams have been graded, the Registrar's office manages the recording and publication of grades. This office is responsible for posting grades so that each student can view their results confidentially through an online portal or the school's designated notification system. It's important to stay alert for these announcements to review your grades and ensure everything is in order.

In case of any discrepancies or if you have questions about your grade, many law schools have policies that allow students to request a review of their exam. This process usually involves meeting with the professor to discuss the grade and receive detailed feedback on your performance. Taking advantage of this opportunity can be extremely beneficial to understand your strengths and areas for improvement and to clarify any misunderstandings about the exam expectations.

It is also crucial to reflect on your post-exam experience, regardless of the results. Analyzing what you did well and what you could improve for future exams is a fundamental part of academic growth. While direct feedback from the professor is valuable, it's also helpful to talk with peers and review your own notes and outlines to identify areas where you could strengthen your understanding and preparation.

In conclusion, the post-exam phase in law school is a structured and meticulous process that ensures fairness and accuracy in evaluation. By understanding and actively participating in this process, you can maximize your learning and continuously improve in your legal studies. Staying informed about how exams and grades are managed, and being willing to seek feedback and clarifications when necessary will help you successfully navigate this critical part of your legal education.

Grading on a Curve in Law School

Grading on a curve is an integral and often controversial aspect of legal education. This evaluation system has significant implications for students, from their academic performance to their professional opportunities. In this section, we will explore what curved grades are, why they are used, how they are implemented, their impacts on students, and the criticisms and debates surrounding them.

Curved grades are an evaluation system in which students' grades are distributed according to a predefined curve, usually following a normal distribution (bell curve). Instead of being based on a fixed scale, students' grades are adjusted in relation to their classmates' performance.

Law schools use curved grades to maintain consistent academic standards and ensure that grades reflect a fair comparison among students. This system helps prevent grade inflation and ensures that only a certain percentage of students receive the highest grades, which can be crucial for distinguishing them in a highly competitive field.

There are several methods for curving grades:

- **Bell Curve:** Distributes grades on a normal curve, with most students receiving grades in the middle range and few receiving the highest and lowest grades.

- **Percentiles:** Assigns grades based on the percentile in which each student falls relative to their peers.

- **Predefined Formulas:** Some institutions use specific formulas to determine grade distribution.

For example, in a large class, a law school might determine that the top 10% of students will receive an A, the next 20% a B, and so on. In smaller classes, the distribution may be adjusted to reflect the sample size and differences in evaluation.

Curved grades can have a significant impact on students' morale and mental health. The pressure to excel in comparison to peers can generate stress and anxiety, affecting emotional well-being. This system fosters a highly competitive environment, where students compete directly with each other for the highest grades. While this can motivate some, it can also create a hostile environment and reduce collaboration. Moreover, curved grades influence employment opportunities, as many law firms and other employers use grades to select candidates. Higher grades can open doors to honors programs, scholarships, and internship opportunities.

Strategies for Navigating Curved Grades

- **Understand the Curve:** Familiarizing yourself with how your school's specific curve works can help you adjust your expectations and study strategies.

- **Effective Study Strategies:** Focus on study techniques that maximize comprehension and retention of material, such as group study and using additional resources.

- **Stress Management:** Adopting stress management practices, such as meditation and exercise, can help you maintain balance during high-pressure periods.

- **Academic Advisors:** Seek support from academic advisors who can offer guidance on how to handle curved grades and improve academic performance.

- **Tutoring Services:** Utilize tutoring services to reinforce understanding of material and better prepare for exams.

Curved grades are a distinctive and debated feature of legal education. Understanding this system and its implications is essential for students to navigate their academic experience and prepare for their future careers. By adopting effective strategies and leveraging available resources, students can better manage the pressure of curved grades and maximize their academic success.

8

SECURING EMPLOYMENT

U p to this point, we have covered everything necessary about the law school experience. Now it's time to focus on a crucial aspect: how to secure a job in the competitive field of law.

The job market for LL.M. students who do not possess a J.D. from a U.S. law school is very competitive. Challenges include visa regulations, the lack of a U.S. J.D., and the inability to take the bar exam in many jurisdictions. It is important for international LL.M. students to understand that these are typical concerns of employers and do not reflect a personal valuation of their skills. Due to these barriers, job hunting for international graduates can be more difficult, and it is essential to start the search as early as possible.

Although less frequent, employers may select LL.M. candidates based on their academic performance, work experience, language skills, licenses in foreign jurisdictions, and specialization in areas of law relevant to the firm's or organization's practice. Given the high competition, it is crucial to be flexible and open-minded about the type of work you will initially accept. Consider the possibility of taking an entry-level position, a non-partnership track position, or employment in a corporation rather than in a law firm. Internships and volunteer opportunities can also provide valuable legal experience in the United States.

Adopt an assertive but not aggressive approach in your job search. You must demonstrate to potential employers that you are highly qualified and can perform the job effectively. Focus on learning how to market your skills and qualifications convincingly.

Employment Under F-1 Visa

International students studying in the United States on an **F-1** visa face unique challenges and diverse opportunities regarding employment during and after their studies. This section explores the different employment options available to F-1 students, highlighting the advantages and requirements associated with each. From on-campus work to Curricular Practical Training (CPT) and Optional Practical Training (OPT), these opportunities not only provide financial support to students but also offer valuable practical experience in their field of study.

On-Campus Employment

One of the first employment options available to F-1 students is working on their educational institution's campus. This type of employment allows students to work up to 20 hours per week during academic periods and full-time during breaks. Most notably, no prior authorization from the international student office or USCIS is required for this type of employment. On-campus work provides students with an excellent opportunity to gain relevant work experience while continuing their studies. In addition to the financial benefits, on-campus employment can help students integrate into the university community, develop communication skills, and build professional networks that can be useful for their future career.

Curricular Practical Training (CPT)

Curricular Practical Training (CPT) is another form of off-campus employment available to F-1 students. This program is designed to allow students to gain practical work experience that is an integral part of their academic curriculum. CPT can include internships, cooperative education programs, or any required practicum sponsored by employers in collaboration with the educational institution. To be eligible for CPT, students must obtain approval from both their academic program and the Office of International Student Services. This type of experience complements theoretical learning with practical applications and can also be crucial for gaining relevant experience in the student's field of study and improving employability after graduation.

To modify the Form I-20 for Curricular Practical Training (CPT), you need to follow a specific process through the Office of International Student Services. First, you must obtain CPT approval through the office so that it is reflected in your Form I-20. This involves providing a letter from the employer with detailed information.

The letter should include your full name, a statement of the job offer, the company's name and address, and the number of hours you will work per week, specifying whether it is full-time or part-time (working more or less than 20 hours per week). It should also include the exact start and end dates of the employment. It is important to note that you technically cannot start working until the CPT form is complete, so you should indicate a future date as the start date, approximately one week after the application date.

Optional Practical Training (OPT)

Optional Practical Training (OPT) is off-campus employment authorization that allows F-1 students to work in their major field of study. Students who have completed at least one full academic year are eligible for up to 12 months of full-time employment for each completed level of study. The months of OPT do not have to be consecutive and can be used before or after graduation. However, any use of OPT before graduation reduces the total available 12 months. Students must apply to the U.S. Citizenship and Immigration Services (USCIS) to obtain OPT authorization, a process that can take between 3 and 5 months. It is essential to start the application process well in advance to avoid interruptions in planned employment after graduation. OPT offers students the opportunity to apply their academic knowledge in real work environments, develop professional skills, and establish connections in their fields of interest.

Employment options under the F-1 visa provide international students with an invaluable platform to develop practical skills, explore their field of study, and prepare for successful careers in the United States. From on-campus employment fostering community integration to CPT and OPT offering relevant work experience, each option plays a crucial role in the academic and professional formation of F-1 students. It is essential for students to take advantage of these opportunities, understand the specific requirements, and prepare adequately to start their professional careers in the competitive U.S. job market.

H-1B Visa Sponsorship

H-1B visa sponsorship is a process through which a U.S. company sponsors a foreign worker to legally work in the country. The H-1B visa is intended for people in specialized occupations that require theoretical and technical knowledge in fields such as computing, engineering, medicine, and others. The U.S. employer must submit a petition for the foreign worker through Form I-129 to the U.S. Citizenship and Immigration Services (USCIS). This petition must include documentation showing that the job requires specialized skills and that the worker possesses the necessary qualifications.

Each year, there is a cap of 85,000 H-1B visas available, of which 20,000 are reserved for people with a master's degree or higher from a U.S. institution. The demand for H-1B visas usually exceeds the supply, so a lottery is conducted to allocate them. The employer must demonstrate that they are offering a fair wage that aligns with local wage standards for the position and must submit an approved "Labor Condition Application" (LCA) to the U.S. Department of Labor. This document ensures that the foreign worker will not negatively affect the working conditions of U.S. workers.

The H-1B visa is initially granted for up to three years and can be renewed for another three years, for a total maximum of six years. In certain cases, additional extensions may be obtained if the worker is in the process of obtaining permanent residency (Green Card). Not all companies are willing to sponsor H-1B visas due to the time, cost, and commitment required. Many companies prefer to avoid this process and opt for candidates who already have permission to work in the United States. It is common for companies to ask candidates during interviews if they will need visa sponsorship in the future to assess their willingness to hire. Indeed, some companies avoid hiring F-1 students on OPT specifically to avoid having to face the H-1B visa sponsorship process later on.

The H-1B visa sponsorship process can be complex and competitive, but it is an important pathway for international lawyers to work and develop professionally in the United States. It is advisable to carefully research and plan this process to increase the chances of success.

The Importance of Networking

Networking is a vital skill for LL.M. students seeking to establish themselves in the competitive legal market. Beyond simply accumulating contacts, networking involves creating solid and meaningful relationships that can open doors to job opportunities, mentorship, and long-term professional development.

From the start of the LL.M. program, actively participating in networking events and activities is crucial. Attending specialized conferences, job fairs, and alumni meetings provides an invaluable platform to interact with legal professionals, learn about current and future market trends, and establish meaningful connections that can lead to concrete professional opportunities.

A fundamental aspect of networking is participation in professional associations and alums groups. These groups offer not only the chance to connect with colleagues and established professionals but also access to educational resources, professional development programs, and exclusive events that can boost your professional growth.

During networking events, it is essential to present yourself effectively. This means clearly communicating your skills, experience, and professional goals in a way that resonates with potential employers and professional contacts. Maintaining a proactive attitude and focusing on establishing genuine relationships can make a difference in how you are perceived within the legal community.

Besides participating in physical events, online networking also plays a crucial role. Platforms like LinkedIn offer the opportunity to connect with legal industry professionals, share relevant posts, participate in discussions, and establish virtual relationships that can translate into job opportunities and professional collaboration.

To maintain effective long-term relationships, it is important to keep cultivating your established connections. This may include regularly sending updates on your academic and professional progress, sharing articles of interest, and maintaining open and constructive communication. Networking is not just about job hunting but about building lasting relationships that can benefit you throughout your professional career.

In summary, effective networking for LL.M. students involves a combination of active participation in physical and virtual events, engagement in relevant professional associations, and the ability to present oneself convincingly and professionally. By investing time and effort in building and maintaining a solid network, you significantly increase your chances of success in the legal market and beyond.

Strategies for Creating an Effective Resume and Cover Letter

Legal resumes in the United States often differ significantly from standards in other countries. Before preparing your resume to send to a U.S. employer, it is crucial to review this section and the provided examples. Your resume is a representation of yourself: your achievements, skills, writing ability, personality, and potential. Most employers spend less than a minute reviewing each resume, and sometimes even less than 30 seconds.

It is essential that your resume highlights your professional strengths and minimizes your weaknesses. There are basic guidelines that students should follow when creating a U.S.-style resume. Below are guidelines on content and format, along with examples of resumes.

The format of a U.S. legal resume is key to catching the employer's attention. A well-organized and visually appealing resume can make a big difference. Use a clear and professional font, such as Times New Roman or Arial, in size 11 or 12. Keep one-inch margins on all sides to ensure the text is not too condensed.

At the top of your resume, include your full name, city, phone number, and email address. Make sure this information is accurate and professional. Avoid unprofessional email addresses. Your name should be in a slightly larger font size to stand out.

Although some resumes include an objective or professional summary, it is generally not recommended to include them in legal resumes, as this is covered in the cover letter. If you wish to use it, it should be brief, one or two sentences, and should focus on your professional intention or highlight your most relevant qualities. For example: "Attorney specialized in international law with experience in litigation and contract negotiation, seeking opportunities to apply skills in a global corporate environment."

The education section should list your academic credentials in reverse chronological order, starting with the most recent degree. Include the name of the institution, location, degree obtained, and graduation date. If you have outstanding grades, such as "cum laude" or "magna cum laude," be sure to mention them. Also, include any relevant scholarships or awards.

Professional experience is one of the most important sections of your resume. List your jobs in reverse chronological order. For each position, include the job title, company name, location, and dates of employment. Below each job, describe your responsibilities and achievements. Be specific and quantify your achievements whenever possible. For example: "Reduced legal costs by 15% through thorough contract review."

You can include a skills section where you highlight your relevant technical and software skills, such as proficiency with LexisNexis, Westlaw, or other legal programs. Also, mention any language skills, especially if you are fluent in more than one language, as this can be very attractive to firms with international clients.

If you have written academic articles or participated in conferences, you can include a publications and presentations section. Mention the title of the article, the journal or conference where it was presented, and the date. This section demonstrates your ability to contribute to the legal field beyond direct practice.

Being a member of legal associations can add significant value to your resume. List all relevant memberships, including the name of the association and your role within it. For example: "Active member of the American Bar Association, International Law Section." Volunteer and extracurricular activities can show your commitment to the community and your ability to work in a team. Briefly describe your role and the activities you performed. For example: "Volunteer at the Immigrant Assistance Legal Clinic, providing free legal advice to asylum seekers." Although it is not necessary to include references directly on your resume, you can indicate that they are available upon request. This is usually done with a simple line at the end of the document: "References available upon request."

Be sure to tailor your resume for each position you apply for. Highlight the most relevant experience and skills for the specific job. Review your resume multiple times to avoid grammatical or formatting errors. Consider asking a colleague or mentor to review it as well. Never include false or exaggerated information. Integrity is fundamental in the legal profession. A well-crafted resume not only opens doors but also represents your first impression on a potential employer. Take the time necessary to polish every detail and ensure it accurately reflects your professionalism and capability.

Now that you have a solid resume that highlights your achievements and skills, the next step is to learn how to write an effective cover letter. While the resume provides an overview of your experience and qualifications, the cover letter is your opportunity to explain in detail why you are the ideal candidate for the position. It is the perfect complement to your resume, allowing you to personalize your message for each employer and highlight specific aspects of your career and personality that make you unique. Below, we will explore how to structure and write a cover letter that captures employers' attention and brings you one step closer to securing the desired job.

The **cover letter** is an essential component of the job search process, especially in the legal field in the United States. It serves as a personal introduction to your resume, allowing you to highlight your skills, experience, and the value you can bring to the organization. An effective cover letter can make the difference between getting an interview and having your application overlooked. Below are the key elements and some tips for writing a cover letter that captures the employer's attention and helps you stand out in the competitive job market.

Begin your cover letter with your contact information at the top, including your name, address, phone number, and email address. Below your information, write the date and then the employer's contact information, including the recipient's name, their title, the company's name, and the company's address. Personalizing the letter with the recipient's name shows your interest and effort in researching the company and the position. If you do not know the recipient's name, a quick search on LinkedIn or the company's website can be helpful.

The first paragraph should immediately grab the reader's attention. Mention the specific position you are applying for and how you learned about the opportunity. If someone recommended the position to you, mention it here. This can include recommendations from colleagues, friends, professors, or even contacts you made through networking events. Additionally, this opening paragraph should give a brief introduction of who you are and why you are interested in the position. For example, you might start with something like: "I am writing to express my interest in the Legal Associate position at [Company Name], advertised on [Source]. As an attorney with experience in [relevant area], I am excited about the opportunity to contribute to your team."

The body of the letter, generally composed of two to three paragraphs, should detail your relevant skills and experience. Explain how your academic background and work experience have prepared you for the position. Use concrete examples to illustrate your achievements and how you have handled similar responsibilities in the past. For example, if you are applying for a position in corporate law, you might mention specific cases where you worked on mergers and acquisitions, highlighting your ability to negotiate and draft complex contracts. Relate your skills to the employer's needs, demonstrating that you understand the position's challenges and are prepared to meet them. Additionally, mention any additional competencies that might be valuable, such as foreign language skills, proficiency with specific legal software, or international experience.

In the next paragraph, discuss why you are particularly attracted to the company. Research the organization's culture, values, and recent projects, and explain how your values and professional goals align with theirs. This shows that you are not just looking for a job but are specifically seeking to work at that company. For example, you might say: "I am particularly impressed by [Company Name]'s commitment to innovation in environmental law. As someone who has worked on sustainability projects, I am excited about the possibility of contributing to your corporate social responsibility initiatives."

The final paragraph should be a call to action. Reiterate your interest in the position and your willingness to discuss your application in an interview. Thank the reader for their time and consideration, and provide your contact details so they can easily reach you. An effective way to close is by saying: "I am very interested in discussing how my skills and experiences can contribute to the success of [Company Name]. Thank you for considering my application. I look forward to the opportunity to speak with you in an interview. You can contact me at [your phone number] or [your email address]."

Close the letter with a professional sign-off, such as "Sincerely," followed by your full name. If you are sending a printed letter, leave space for your signature between the sign-off and your typed name. For email submissions, simply type your name after the sign-off.

Remember to review and proofread your cover letter to ensure it is free of grammatical and typographical errors. A well-written and error-free letter reflects your attention to detail and professionalism. Additionally, keep the cover letter concise and to the point; ideally, it should not exceed one page. Use clear and professional language, and avoid using jargon or overly technical terms that the employer may not understand.

Moreover, tailor each cover letter to the specific job you are applying for. Although it may be tempting to use a generic cover letter, a personalized letter shows that you have taken the time and effort to understand the employer's needs and how you can meet them.

Other Documents to Know When Applying

When applying for a job in the legal field in the United States, besides the resume and cover letter, employers may request additional documents. These can include writing samples, academic transcripts, and references. Each of these documents plays a crucial role in the selection process, providing employers with a more comprehensive view of your skills, experience, and academic background. Below, we detail the importance of each and how to prepare them adequately.

Writing samples are essential in the application process for many legal positions. These samples demonstrate your ability to draft clear, precise, and well-founded legal documents, which is a fundamental skill for any attorney. When selecting a writing sample, choose a work that reflects your best writing and is relevant to the position you are applying for. This could be a legal memo, an excerpt from a law review note, a court motion, or any other document you have prepared during your studies or work experience. It is crucial that the sample is your own work and not a team collaboration. If the original document is lengthy, you can provide an excerpt, ensuring to include an explanatory note that provides context about the complete document. Carefully review your writing sample to avoid grammatical and typographical errors, and ensure it is written in a professional style that meets legal standards.

Academic transcripts are another critical component of the application process. These transcripts provide employers with a detailed view of your academic performance throughout your educational career. They include a list of the courses you have taken, the grades you have received, and, in some cases, your overall grade point average (GPA). When applying for a job in the legal field, it is important to request an official copy of your transcripts from all educational institutions you have attended. Ensure you request these transcripts well in advance, as some institutions may take several weeks to process and send these documents. Keep a digital copy of your official transcripts to easily send them to employers who require them.

References are also crucial in the job search process. Employers often request references to gain an external perspective on your skills, work ethic, and professionalism. Carefully select your references, choosing individuals who can speak positively and specifically about your capabilities and achievements. References can include former employers, professors, colleagues, or supervisors with whom you have worked closely. Before listing someone as a reference, ensure you obtain their permission and provide them with information about the position you are applying for so they can prepare an appropriate recommendation. It is helpful to provide your references with a copy of your resume and details about the job for which you are being considered, so they can tailor their comments to the skills and experiences most relevant to the position.

In summary, when preparing your application for a legal position, it is essential to include a high-quality writing sample, official academic transcripts, and solid references. These additional documents provide employers with a more comprehensive view of your professional and academic profile and can be decisive in the selection process. Be sure to carefully review and prepare each of these components to present a strong and professional application.

Pro Bono Work for Admission

In many jurisdictions in the United States, aspiring bar applicants are required to complete a specific number of **pro bono** hours before they can practice law. This requirement underscores the importance of community service and the commitment to social justice in the legal profession. Taking advantage of pro bono opportunities during your time in law school will not only help you meet this requirement but also enrich your educational and professional experience.

Pro bono work, which refers to providing free legal services to individuals or communities who cannot afford such services, is a valuable way to gain practical experience. Engaging in pro bono activities allows you to apply the knowledge gained in the classroom to real-world situations, improve your legal skills, and build confidence in your ability to help others. Additionally, pro bono work provides the opportunity to explore different areas of law and develop a deeper understanding of the various legal needs of the community.

Most law schools in the United States offer a variety of pro bono opportunities through their legal clinics, externship programs, and partnerships with nonprofit organizations. These opportunities are designed to be accessible and flexible, allowing you to fulfill your academic obligations while gaining practical experience. It is advisable to familiarize yourself with the pro bono programs available at your institution from the beginning of your studies, so you can plan how to incorporate these activities into your academic schedule.

Engaging in pro bono work not only fulfills bar admission requirements but also demonstrates your commitment to social justice to future employers. Many law firms and organizations value candidates who have dedicated time and effort to pro bono activities, as this reflects an ethic of service and a dedication to responsible legal practice. Moreover, pro bono hours can serve as a valuable addition to your resume and can be a significant topic to discuss during job interviews.

To maximize the benefit of your pro bono work, it is useful to keep a detailed record of the hours you dedicate to these activities, as well as the types of cases and projects you participate in. Some jurisdictions require the submission of specific documentation when applying for bar admission, so maintaining an organized record will facilitate this process. Reflecting on your pro bono experiences and considering how they have influenced your professional and personal development is also beneficial.

In summary, completing pro bono hours during your time in law school is an excellent way to meet bar admission requirements, gain practical experience, and demonstrate your commitment to community service. Take advantage of the pro bono opportunities available at your institution to develop your legal skills, explore different areas of law, and contribute positively to the community. By doing so, you will not only fulfill an essential requirement but also enrich your legal education and better prepare yourself for a successful and meaningful career in law.

Sample Resume

NAME SURNAME
City, State Abbreviation - Mobile Phone - Email Address

BAR STATUS

Plan to take the Uniform Bar Exam for admission in the State of X, Date

EDUCATION

LAW SCHOOL, City, State Abbreviation, Country
Candidate for LL.M. in _, Expected Month 20__
Honors: Honor Name
Activities: Activity, Title
LAW SCHOOL, City, State Abbreviation, Country
Degree Abbreviation, Month 20__
Honors: Honor Name
Activities: Activity, Title
SCHOOL, City, State Abbreviation, Country
Degree Abbreviation, Month 20__
Honors: Honor Name
Activities: Activity, Title

EXPERIENCE

EMPLOYER NAME, City, State Abbreviation
Title, Month 20__ – Month 20__
Description.
EMPLOYER NAME, City, State Abbreviation
Title, Month 20__ – Month 20__
Description.
EMPLOYER NAME, City, State Abbreviation
Title, Month 20__ – Month 20__
Description.

ADDITIONAL INFORMATION

Languages, interests, certifications, others.

Sample Cover Letter

NAME SURNAME
City, State Abbreviation - Mobile Phone - Email Address

[Date]

VIA: E-MAIL
[Recruiter's Name]
[Recruiter's Title]
[Company Name]
[Company Address]
Mu[City, State, Zip Code]
Dear [Recruiter's Name]:

I am writing to express my interest in the position of [Job Title] advertised in [Where You Found the Offer]. I recently obtained my LL.M. degree from [Name of the U.S. Law School] and am a law graduate from [Name of the Foreign Law School]. I am very excited about the opportunity to apply my legal knowledge and skills at [Company Name].

During my time at [Name of the U.S. Law School], I specialized in [Specialization Area], where I gained a strong foundation in [Mention a Relevant Skill]. In my previous experience at [Previous Employer Name], I worked as [Job Title], developing skills in [Mention a Specific Task or Skill]. These experiences have prepared me to contribute effectively to your team. I was drawn to this position at [Company Name] because of its reputation in [Mention Something Specific About the Company]. I believe my education and experience allow me to bring a unique and valuable perspective to your team.

Attached to this letter is my resume. I look forward to discussing how my skills and experiences can contribute to the success of [Company Name]. Thank you for your time and consideration, and I hope to have the opportunity to speak with you in an interview.

Sincerely,
[Name] [Surname]

9

DIFFERENT EXAMS FOR ADMISSION

S o far, we have covered in detail all the necessary aspects to successfully complete law school. We have explored admission requirements, different types of student visas, how to prepare and submit your applications, and strategies for maintaining good academic performance during your studies. Additionally, we have discussed the importance of financial planning, including how to obtain funding and scholarships to support your studies in the United States.

As we have seen, the legal profession in the United States is one of the most respected and demanding, requiring a solid academic background and a deep commitment to ethics and professionalism. To practice as an attorney in any U.S. jurisdiction, you must pass a series of standardized exams that evaluate both theoretical knowledge and practical skills. These exams ensure that all lawyers have the necessary competence to effectively represent their clients and meet the high standards of the profession.

In this chapter, we will explore in detail the different exams you need to pass to obtain a law license in various U.S. jurisdictions. From the rigorous Bar Exam to specific tests like the Multistate Professional Responsibility Examination (MPRE), each exam plays a crucial role in preparing future lawyers for the challenges of legal practice. We will also examine additional exams required in certain specialties and jurisdictions, as well as preparation strategies to help you face these challenges with confidence.

This chapter will provide you with a comprehensive understanding of the requirements needed to be admitted as a lawyer, ensuring you are well-prepared to embark on your legal career in the United States.

Multistate Professional Responsibility Examination (MPRE)

The **Multistate Professional Responsibility Examination (MPRE)** is a crucial component on the path to becoming a licensed attorney in the United States. Administered by the National Conference of Bar Examiners (NCBE), this exam is required by most jurisdictions to ensure that future lawyers understand and respect the standards of professional conduct and ethics.

The MPRE is designed to assess your knowledge and understanding of the ethical rules and professional conduct that govern the practice of law. Unlike the Bar Exam, which measures substantive legal knowledge, the MPRE focuses on ethical rules based on the **American Bar Association's (ABA) Model Rules of Professional Conduct**, as well as other standards and judicial precedents related to professional ethics.

The exam consists of 60 multiple-choice questions that you must complete in a two-hour period. Of these 60 questions, 50 are scored, and the remaining 10 are pre-tested for future exams and do not affect your score. The questions cover various areas of professional ethics, including conflicts of interest, confidentiality, advertising and solicitation, competence, responsibilities of lawyers and judges, and conduct in litigation.

Most U.S. jurisdictions require passing the MPRE as part of the process to obtain a license to practice law. However, minimum score requirements may vary by jurisdiction. Generally, a score between 75 and 85 is sufficient to pass, but it is crucial to check the specific requirements of the jurisdiction where you plan to practice.

Passing the MPRE is not only a requirement for obtaining a license in many jurisdictions but also a sign of your commitment to professional ethics and responsible conduct in the practice of law. The ability to understand and apply ethical rules is fundamental to protecting clients' interests, maintaining the integrity of the legal profession, and ensuring justice in the legal system.

The MPRE, though specific in its focus, is an integral part of the process of forming a competent and ethical lawyer. By dedicating the necessary time and effort to prepare for and pass this exam, you will be taking a crucial step toward a successful and respected legal career.

Preparation Strategies for the MPRE

Preparing for the Multistate Professional Responsibility Examination (MPRE) requires a combination of disciplined study and familiarity with the types of questions that will be presented on the exam. Here are some key strategies to ensure successful performance:

1. Enroll in a Preparation Course: Most bar prep programs offer free courses specifically for the MPRE. These courses usually include video lessons, practice quizzes, and exam simulations. Some of the most well-known providers are Barbri, Kaplan, and Themis. Enrolling in one of these courses can provide valuable structure and resources for your study.

2. Review the Professional Conduct Model Rules: The MPRE is primarily based on the American Bar Association's (ABA) Model Rules of Professional Conduct. Make sure to thoroughly read and understand this document, as many exam questions will assess your knowledge and application of these rules.

3. Practice with Previous Exams: Taking practice exams is one of the most effective ways to prepare for the MPRE. These exams familiarize you with the question format and the type of reasoning expected. They also help you identify areas where you need improvement. Take advantage of question banks provided by prep courses and practice regularly to develop your ability to analyze and answer questions efficiently.

4. Establish a Study Schedule: MPRE preparation should be a structured process. Create a study schedule that allows you to cover all exam content areas with enough time to review and reinforce the most challenging concepts. Dedicating specific daily or weekly study time can help keep you on track.

5. Utilize Additional Resources: Besides prep courses and practice exams, many other resources are available to help you prepare for the MPRE. Study books, mobile apps, and online guides can provide detailed explanations of concepts and additional practice questions. Consider joining study groups or online forums where you can discuss difficult questions and share strategies with other students preparing for the same exam.

6. Exam Techniques and Time Management: The MPRE has a time limit, so it is essential to develop good time management skills. Practice answering questions within a set timeframe to get used to the pressure of the actual exam. Learn to read each question carefully and quickly eliminate incorrect options to increase your chances of selecting the correct answer.

By implementing these preparation strategies, you can significantly increase your chances of success on the MPRE. Remember that consistency and practice are key to mastering the material and feeling confident on exam day.

Jurisdiction-Specific Passing Scores

To obtain a license to practice law in a specific jurisdiction, it is crucial to understand the Multistate Professional Responsibility Examination (MPRE) score requirements for that region. Each jurisdiction has its own minimum passing score, which can vary significantly. The following table details the minimum scores required to pass the MPRE in different U.S. jurisdictions. This information is essential for planning your preparation and ensuring you meet the necessary standards for the jurisdiction where you wish to practice.[17]

Jurisdiction	Passing score
Alabama	75
Alaska	80
Arizona	85
Arkansas	85
California	86
Colorado	85
Connecticut	80
Delaware	85
District of Columbia	75
Florida	80
Georgia	75

---

[17] Information taken from the National Conference of Bar Examiners; it is important to verify the specific requirements at the time of application. Available at https://reports.ncbex.org/comp-guide/charts/chart-6/#mpre

Hawaii	85
Idaho	85
Illinois	80
Indiana	80
Iowa	80
Kansas	80
Kentucky	80
Louisiana	80
Maine	80
Maryland	85
Massachusetts	85
Michigan	85
Minnesota	85
Mississippi	75
Missouri	80
Montana	80
Nebraska	85
Nevada	85
New Hampshire	79
New Jersey	75
New Mexico	80
New York	85
North Carolina	80
North Dakota	85
Ohio	85
Oklahoma	80
Oregon	85
Pennsylvania	75
Rhode Island	80
South Carolina	77
South Dakota	85
Tennessee	82
Texas	85
Utah	86
Vermont	80
Virginia	85
Virgin Islands	75
Washington	85

West Virginia	80
Wisconsin	Not necessary
Wyoming	85

Sections of the MPRE

The MPRE exam is structured into several sections that cover different aspects of professional ethics and responsibility in legal practice. These sections are designed to assess your knowledge and understanding of the rules governing the conduct of lawyers. Below are the sections of the MPRE, each focusing on specific areas crucial to practicing law with integrity and professionalism:[18]

Section	Percentage
Regulation of the Legal Profession	6-12%
The Client-Lawyer Relationship	10-16%
Client Confidentiality	6-12%
Conflicts of Interest	12-18%
Competence, Malpractice, and Other Civil Liability	6-12%
Litigation and Other Forms of Advocacy	10-16%
Transactions and Communications with Non-Clients	2-8%
Different Roles of the Lawyer	4-10%
Safekeeping Funds and Other Property	2-8%
Communications About Legal Services	4-10%
Lawyer's Duties to the Public and the Legal System	2-4%
Judicial Conduct	2-8%

---

[18] The National Conference of Bar Examiners provides a more detailed outline, available at https://www.ncbex.org/sites/default/files/2023-01/MPRE_Subject_Matter_Outline.pdf

Uniform Bar Exam

The **Uniform Bar Exam (UBE)** is a standardized assessment created by the **National Conference of Bar Examiners (NCBE)** and is used in many jurisdictions across the United States. The primary goal of the UBE is to provide a uniform measure of essential skills and knowledge for legal practice. This standardization allows the scores obtained in the exam to be transferable among the jurisdictions that have adopted the UBE, facilitating the professional mobility of lawyers within the country. [19]

The adoption of the UBE by various jurisdictions has revolutionized the way new lawyers obtain their licenses to practice. Previously, lawyers had to take state-specific exams, complicating the process of relocation and practice in multiple states. With the UBE, a uniform score can be accepted in any participating jurisdiction, significantly simplifying this process.

Although the UBE provides a standardized measure of general legal competencies, individual jurisdictions may have additional requirements. These can include tests on specific state laws or additional educational components to ensure that candidates are familiar with the legal particulars of the jurisdiction where they seek admission.

The main objective of the UBE is to assess the fundamental knowledge and skills that all lawyers must possess before being licensed to practice law. The portability of the UBE score is a significant advantage, allowing candidates to use their scores to apply for admission in any of the jurisdictions that accept the UBE. This flexibility benefits both examinees, who gain greater professional mobility, and jurisdictions, which receive a standardized measure of candidate competency.

The relevance of the UBE can be highlighted in several aspects:

1. Score Portability: The ability to transfer scores between states provides great flexibility for lawyers seeking to work in different jurisdictions without needing to take multiple bar exams. This is particularly beneficial for those in metropolitan areas spanning multiple states or those looking to relocate for personal or professional reasons.

2. Standardized Evaluation: By providing a standardized exam, the UBE ensures that all candidates are assessed under the same criteria and standards, regardless of jurisdiction. This promotes an equitable basis for measuring the competency of aspiring lawyers.

---

[19] Information adapted from the National Conference of Bar Examiners, available at https://www.ncbex.org/exams/ube/about-ube

3. Reduction of Costs and Efforts: The UBE reduces the need to prepare for and take multiple state-specific exams, saving time and money for applicants. This efficiency also extends to jurisdictions, which can focus on other aspects of licensing and regulating the profession.

4. Promotion of National Competence: By unifying the evaluation process, the UBE fosters healthy competition among lawyers at the national level, ensuring that essential skills and knowledge are recognized and valued uniformly across all participating states.

Jurisdictions that Have Adopted the UBE

The Uniform Bar Examination (UBE) has been adopted by a significant number of jurisdictions in the United States, reflecting a trend towards standardization and portability of law licenses. These jurisdictions recognize the advantages of a uniform exam, allowing aspiring lawyers to transfer their scores and practice in multiple states without the need to retake the bar exam. Below, we present a detailed list of the jurisdictions that have adopted the UBE, highlighting the positive impact of this adoption on the professional mobility of lawyers and the consistency in evaluating legal competencies nationwide. [20]

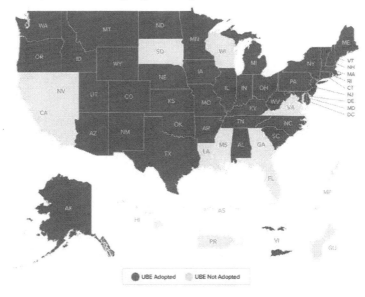

---

[20] Map created by Legal UWorld, available at https://legal.uworld.com/bar-exam/states/

Components of the UBE

The **Uniform Bar Examination (UBE)** is a comprehensive evaluation consisting of three main components designed to comprehensively measure the skills and knowledge necessary for legal practice. Each of these components—**the Multistate Essay Examination (MEE), the Multistate Performance Test (MPT),** and **the Multistate Bar Examination (MBE)**—contributes to a complete and uniform assessment of aspiring lawyers' competence. Below, each of these components is broken down, explaining their structure, purpose, and how they are administered within the context of the UBE.

Multistate Performance Test (MPT)

The **Multistate Performance Test (MPT)** consists of two 90-minute exercises each, developed by the National Conference of Bar Examiners (NCBE). These exercises are administered in jurisdictions participating in the bar exam on the Tuesday before the last Wednesday of February and July each year. Jurisdictions may choose to include one or both MPT exercises in their exams. Those administering the Uniform Bar Examination (UBE) use both MPT exercises.[21]

The MPT is just one of several tools that a bar examiners committee may employ to evaluate the competence of legal practice aspirants. Each jurisdiction grades the MPT and establishes its own policy regarding the weight it is given compared to other exam components. Jurisdictions administering the UBE assign the MPT a weight of 20%.

The MPT aims to evaluate the examinee's ability to use fundamental advocacy skills in realistic situations and complete tasks that a novice lawyer should be able to perform. It is not a test of specific legal knowledge, but an assessment of essential skills that lawyers are expected to demonstrate regardless of their practice area.

The MPT consists of two 90-minute tasks. The materials for each task include a File and a Library. The File contains source documents with all the case facts and a description of the specific task the examinee must complete, provided in a supervising attorney's memorandum. The File may include interview transcripts, statements, hearings or trials, pleadings, correspondence, client documents, contracts, newspaper articles, medical

---

[21] Adapted from the MPT section of the National Conference of Bar Examiners, available at https://www.ncbex.org/exams/mpt/about-mpt

records, police reports, or attorney notes. Relevant and irrelevant facts are included, and these may be ambiguous, incomplete, or contradictory. Similar to real practice, a client's or supervising attorney's version of the facts may be incomplete or unreliable. Examinees are expected to identify when facts are inconsistent or missing and determine additional sources of information.[22]

The Library may contain cases, statutes, regulations, or rules, some of which may not be relevant to the assigned task. Examinees are expected to extract from the Library the legal principles necessary to analyze the problem and perform the task. The MPT is not a substantive test of law; the materials in the Library provide enough substantive information to complete the task.

The MPT evaluates various essential advocacy skills, including: (1) sorting detailed factual materials and separating relevant facts from irrelevant ones; (2) analyzing legal materials, such as statutes and cases, to extract applicable legal principles; (3) applying the relevant law to relevant facts to resolve a client's problem; (4) identifying and resolving ethical dilemmas when they are present; (5) communicating effectively in writing; and (6) completing an advocacy task within a limited time.

These skills are tested by requiring examinees to perform one or more of a variety of legal tasks. For example, examinees could be instructed to complete tasks such as: a memorandum for a supervising attorney, a letter to a client, a memorandum or persuasive writing, a statement of facts, a contract clause, a will, a counseling plan, a settlement proposal, a discovery plan, a witness examination plan or a final argument.

The MPT examines other fundamental advocacy skills necessary for the completion of many legal tasks.[23] These skills include:

1. Problem-solving: The examinee must demonstrate the ability to develop and evaluate strategies to solve a problem or achieve a goal, including identifying and diagnosing the problem, generating alternative solutions, developing and implementing an action plan, and maintaining the planning process open to new information and ideas.

2. Legal analysis and reasoning: The examinee must demonstrate the ability to analyze and apply legal rules and principles, including

---

[22] Adapted from the MPT preparation section of the National Conference of Bar Examiners, available at https://www.ncbex.org/exams/mpt/preparing-mpt
[23] Adapted from "MPT skills tested" by the National Conference of Bar Examiners, available at https://www.ncbex.org/sites/default/files/2023-01/MPT_Skills_Tested_2023.pdf

identifying and formulating legal issues, identifying relevant legal rules, formulating, developing, and evaluating legal theories, and synthesizing legal arguments.

3. Factual analysis: The examinee must demonstrate the ability to analyze and use facts, plan and direct factual research, including identifying relevant facts, determining the need for factual research, planning research, organizing information, and evaluating collected information.

4. Communication: The examinee must demonstrate the ability to communicate effectively in writing, evaluating the perspective of the communication's recipient and organizing and expressing ideas accurately, clearly, logically, and economically.

5. Organization and management of a legal task: The examinee must demonstrate the ability to organize and manage a legal task, allocating time, effort, and resources efficiently and completing tasks within time constraints.

6. Recognition and resolution of ethical dilemmas: The examinee must demonstrate the ability to represent a client consistently with applicable ethical standards, including knowledge of the nature and sources of ethical standards, the means by which these standards are applied, and the ability to recognize and resolve ethical dilemmas.

The evaluation of these skills ensures that aspiring lawyers not only have theoretical knowledge of the law, but also are able to apply this knowledge practically in real situations.

Preparing for the Multistate Performance Test (MPT) requires a strategic approach, as this section of the exam does not evaluate substantive legal knowledge, but the practical skills that lawyers use in their daily work. Below are effective techniques and strategies to prepare for the MPT:

1. Familiarize yourself with the MPT format: Before you start studying, make sure you fully understand the MPT format. Review examples of past exams and model answers provided by the National Conference of Bar Examiners (NCBE). Familiarizing yourself with the structure of the File and Library, as well as the types of documents you might encounter, will help you feel more comfortable on exam day.

2. Develop time management skills: The MPT requires you to complete each task in 90 minutes. Practice effectively managing your time by properly dividing time between reading materials, planning your response, and writing. A good rule of thumb is to spend approximately

45 minutes reading and planning, and the remaining 45 minutes writing. Conduct timed simulations to improve your ability to complete tasks within the time limit.

3. Practice reading and analyzing documents: The MPT includes a variety of documents in the File and Library. Practice reading and analyzing these documents to identify relevant facts, extract applicable legal principles, and plan your response. Focus on separating relevant from irrelevant facts and identifying any inconsistencies or ambiguities in the provided information.

4. Improve your writing skills: The MPT evaluates your ability to communicate effectively in writing. Practice drafting different types of legal documents that you might encounter in the MPT, such as memoranda, client letters, persuasive writings, statements of facts, and counseling plans. Focus on organizing and expressing your ideas clearly, accurately, and logically. Receive feedback on your writing and work on improving your weaknesses.

5. Use preparation resources: Take advantage of available preparation resources, such as bar preparation courses that offer specific sessions for the MPT. Most bar exam preparation programs offer free MPT preparation courses, which provide practice exercises, study strategies, and writing guides. Using these resources can give you a significant advantage in your preparation.

6. Simulate exam day: Conduct full simulations of the MPT under exam conditions. Simulate the exam environment as faithfully as possible, including time constraints and the type of materials provided. This practice will help you get used to the pace of the exam and reduce anxiety on the actual exam day.

7. Review and learn from past mistakes: After each practice exercise, review your answers compared to model answers. Identify your mistakes and areas for improvement. Learning from your past mistakes will allow you to adjust your approach and continuously improve.

Implementing these preparation techniques will help you develop the skills necessary to perform well on the MPT and increase your chances of success on the bar exam.

Multistate Essay Examination (MEE)

The **Multistate Essay Examination (MEE)** is a key tool used by bar examiners boards in various jurisdictions to assess the competence of aspiring lawyers. This exam, developed by the National Conference of

Bar Examiners (NCBE), is part of the Uniform Bar Examination (UBE), which is uniformly administered in participating jurisdictions on the Tuesday before the last Wednesday of February and July each year.[24]

The primary purpose of the MEE is to assess examinees' ability to identify and analyze legal issues from hypothetical situations. MEE essays not only measure substantive legal knowledge but also the ability to separate relevant from irrelevant information, and to present reasoned analysis clearly, concisely, and well-organized. This exam is crucial to demonstrate written communication skills, an essential competency for any practicing lawyer.

The MEE consists of six essay questions, each of which must be answered within a 30-minute timeframe. The areas of law that may be covered in the MEE are diverse and include:[25]

- **Business organizations:** Includes topics of Agency, Partnership, Corporations, and Limited Liability Companies.

- **Civil procedure:** Addresses aspects related to the judicial process.

- **Conflict of laws:** Deals with the application of laws from different jurisdictions in legal cases.

- **Constitutional law:** Examines issues of constitutional interpretation and fundamental rights.

- **Contracts:** Includes common law of contracts and Article 2 of the Uniform Commercial Code (UCC) on sales.

- **Criminal law and procedure:** Covers principles of criminal law and criminal judicial process.

- **Evidence:** Focuses on rules of admissibility of evidence in judicial proceedings.

- **Family law:** Includes topics such as marriage, divorce, custody, and child support.

- **Property:** Examines aspects of rights in real estate and personal property.

- **Torts:** Addresses civil liability and damages.

- **Trusts and estates:** Includes estates, wills, and trusts.

- **Article 9 of the UCC:** Refers to secured transactions.

The MEE is one of the three components of the UBE, along with the Multistate Bar Examination (MBE) and the Multistate Performance

---

[24] Adapted from the MEE section of the National Conference of Bar Examiners, available at https://www.ncbex.org/exams/mee/about-mee

[25] Covered topics available at https://www.ncbex.org/exams/mee/preparing-mee

Test (MPT). In jurisdictions that administer the UBE, the MEE represents 30% of the total exam score. This significant weighting underscores the importance of writing and analytical skills in legal practice. Through the MEE, examiners can assess not only the examinees' knowledge across various legal areas but also their ability to apply this knowledge practically and effectively.

To effectively prepare for the MEE, it is essential to develop a series of strategies:

1. Deep understanding of substantive law: Ensure you have a solid knowledge of the areas of law that may be examined. This includes not only legal rules but also the ability to apply them to hypothetical situations.

2. Essay writing practice: Regular practice of writing essays under timed conditions can significantly enhance your organizational and analytical skills. Use questions from past exams to familiarize yourself with the format and expectations.

3. Analysis of past questions: Review and analyze questions from previous exams to identify common patterns and recurring areas. This will help you focus on the most relevant topics and understand how questions are structured.

4. Feedback and revision: Obtain feedback on your essays from mentors, professors, or peers. Critical review of your responses can help identify weaknesses and areas for improvement.

5. Time management: Practice responding to questions within the allotted time to ensure you can complete each essay within the 30 minutes available.

The MEE is a comprehensive assessment that measures both legal knowledge and practical skills of future lawyers. Through diligent and strategic preparation, examinees can develop the necessary competencies to excel in this crucial component of the UBE and progress in their path toward professional legal practice.

Multistate Bar Examination (MBE).

The **Multistate Bar Examination (MBE)** is a fundamental part of the Uniform Bar Examination (UBE) and one of the most recognized components of bar admission exams in the United States. Administered by the National Conference of Bar Examiners (NCBE), the MBE assesses the essential knowledge and skills that a practicing attorney must possess.

The purpose of the MBE is to provide a standardized measure of the basic skills and legal knowledge that are fundamental to the practice of law. This multiple-choice exam is designed to evaluate candidates' ability to apply legal principles to hypothetical situations. Unlike the MEE essays, the MBE does not measure written communication skills but instead focuses on the analysis and application of substantive law. It assesses to what extent an examinee can apply fundamental legal principles and legal reasoning to analyze given factual situations.

The MBE consists of 200 multiple-choice questions to be completed in a single day, specifically on the last Wednesday of February and July.[26] The exam is divided into two sessions of three hours each, with 100 questions per session. MBE questions are divided into seven main areas of law, each with 25 scored questions:[27]

1. Constitutional Law: Examines government principles and structures, as well as individual rights and liberties.

2. Contracts: Includes topics from common law contracts and Article 2 of the Uniform Commercial Code (UCC) on sales.

3. Criminal Law and Procedure: Covers substantive criminal laws and criminal judicial process.

4. Evidence: Focuses on rules governing the admissibility of evidence in judicial proceedings.

5. Torts: Covers compensation for damages and civil liability.

6. Real Property: Examines rights in real estate and personal property.

7. Civil Procedure: Includes aspects of judicial process and litigation.

In addition to these 175 scored questions, the MBE includes 25 pretest questions that are not scored but are randomly mixed with the others. Therefore, examinees must attempt all questions.

In the context of the UBE, the MBE represents 50% of the total exam score. This significant weighting underscores the importance of having a solid knowledge base and the ability to apply legal principles across a wide range of legal areas. MBE scores are portable, allowing candidates to transfer their results to any jurisdiction that accepts the UBE, providing professional flexibility and mobility.

To effectively prepare for the MBE, it is crucial to adopt several strategies:

1. Structured Study: Organize a study plan covering all examined areas of law. Use reliable study materials and follow a disciplined schedule.

---

[26] Adapted from the general explanation provided by the National Conference of Bar Examiners at https://www.ncbex.org/exams/mbe/about-mbe

[27] Topics available at https://www.ncbex.org/exams/mbe/preparing-mbe

2. Regular Practice: Solve practice questions regularly to become familiar with the exam format and improve your ability to respond under time pressure. Use question banks and full-length practice exams.

3. Review Key Concepts: Ensure understanding and ability to apply fundamental legal concepts in each area of law. Repetition and constant review are key to consolidating knowledge.

4. Analyze Incorrect Answers: Analyze incorrect answers to identify error patterns and areas needing more attention. This will help correct weaknesses and improve performance.

5. Time Management Techniques: Practice completing questions within the allocated time to improve speed and accuracy. Learning to manage time effectively during the exam is crucial to ensuring you can answer all questions.

6. Use Preparation Courses: Consider enrolling in MBE preparation courses that offer practice exams, study materials, and review sessions. Many of these courses also include specific strategies for addressing multiple-choice questions.

The MBE evaluates a variety of essential skills for legal practice, including:

1. Understanding and Application of Law: The ability to interpret and apply legal principles to specific factual situations.

2. Legal Analysis and Reasoning: The skill to analyze facts and formulate strong legal arguments.

3. Recognition of Legal Dilemmas: Competence to identify relevant legal issues within a factual context.

4. Decision Making Under Pressure: The ability to make quick and accurate decisions in a timed exam environment.

During the MBE, examinees have three hours in each session to answer all questions. There are no scheduled breaks during the morning and afternoon sessions. It is essential that examinees mark all their answers on the answer sheet within the allotted time limit. No marks or corrections are allowed once the end of the time is announced. Scores are based on the number of correct answers, with no penalty for incorrect answers.

The MBE is a rigorous and challenging assessment tool that requires intensive and focused preparation. Through meticulous study and consistent practice, candidates can develop the necessary competencies to succeed in this critical component of the UBE and advance their path toward bar admission and professional legal practice.

NextGen Bar Exam

The **NextGen Bar Exam**, a significant innovation in assessing legal competence, will be launched in a limited number of U.S. jurisdictions in July 2026. This exam is designed to evaluate a variety of essential skills for attorneys, using a focused set of fundamental legal concepts and principles necessary in current legal practice.

Starting in July 2026, the NextGen Bar Exam will consistently evaluate family law, trusts, and estates through performance tasks and integrated question sets, providing legal resources for these concepts. Starting in July 2028, these topics will be integrated into the exam in the same manner as other essential legal concepts, such as business associations, civil procedure, constitutional law, contract law, criminal law, evidence, real property, and torts. [28]

The NextGen Bar Exam focuses not only on knowledge of legal principles but also on a wide range of practical skills essential for effective legal practice. These skills include:

- **Legal Research:** Ability to find and use relevant legal sources.
- **Legal Writing:** Competence to draft clear and effective legal documents.
- **Problem Identification and Analysis:** Ability to identify legal issues and analyze them appropriately.
- **Research and Evaluation:** Critical evaluation of information and evidence.
- **Client Counseling:** Providing clear and useful advice to clients.
- **Negotiation and Dispute Resolution:** Effective handling of negotiations and conflict resolutions.
- **Client Relationship and Management:** Maintaining effective relationships with clients and managing their expectations and needs.

The NextGen Bar Exam will be administered and graded by individual U.S. jurisdictions, with the NCBE providing the technological platform for scoring. The exam will be conducted on examinees' laptops at supervised testing locations. A secure online assessment platform will be used to administer the exam and collect responses. This platform will offer assistive technologies and customized formats for those requiring accommodations.

---

[28] All information has been adapted from official information from the National Conference of Bar Examiners, available at https://www.ncbex.org/exams/nextgen/about-nextgen

The NextGen Exam will replace the current Uniform Bar Examination (UBE) as the basis for score portability between participating jurisdictions. During the transition period, UBE jurisdictions will accept both current UBE scores and NextGen scores for portability purposes, with current UBE scores remaining valid for the time limit set by each jurisdiction.

The NextGen Bar Exam will use a variety of question types to assess examinees:

- **Multiple-Choice Questions:** Approximately 40% of exam time, with four to six answer choices and one or more correct answers. Initially, these will resemble questions from the Multistate Bar Examination (MBE).

- **Integrated Question Sets:** Approximately a quarter of exam time. Based on a common set of factual scenarios, these may include legal resources and supplementary documents, blending multiple-choice questions with short-answer questions.

- **Performance Tasks:** Approximately one-third of exam time. Require examinees to demonstrate fundamental skills in realistic situations, completing tasks typical of a novice attorney.

The NextGen Exam will be implemented in phases over several years, starting in July 2026. The first jurisdictions to adopt the exam will be:[29]

- **July 2026:** Connecticut, Guam, Maryland, Missouri, Oregon, Washington

- **July 2027:** Arizona, Iowa, Kentucky, Minnesota, Nebraska, New Mexico, Oklahoma, Tennessee, Vermont, Wyoming

- **July 2028:** Colorado, Kansas, Utah

The NextGen Bar Exam represents a significant advancement in assessing legal competence, adapting to the evolving needs of legal practice and ensuring that new attorneys are well-prepared to face the challenges of their profession.

Other State Exams

In addition to the Uniform Bar Examination (UBE) and the NextGen Bar Exam, several states in the United States administer their own state-specific bar exams for admission to the bar. These exams reflect the legal and regulatory peculiarities of each jurisdiction and can vary significantly in format, content, and requirements.

---

[29] These dates are still tentative, so it is necessary to keep checking official sources to know when new jurisdictions will be adopting it.

Each state that has not adopted the UBE establishes its own exam requirements, which may include a combination of multiple-choice questions, essays, and performance tasks. In addition to these general components, many states have specific sections covering particular areas of law specific to the jurisdiction. For example, some states may require detailed knowledge of state law, local laws, or specific regulations not covered in the UBE.

States like California, Florida, and Louisiana, among others, administer their own bar exams that include specific sections tailored to their legal needs. These exams may be known for their rigor and the need for specific preparation for the legal peculiarities of the state.

For those seeking licensure to practice law in a state that does not participate in the UBE, it is crucial to research and understand the specific requirements of that jurisdiction. Aspirants should confirm exam details, including the components to be tested, recommended study resources, and any additional courses or exams required to meet the state's admission standards.

In summary, the diversity of state exams in the United States underscores the importance of detailed and specific preparation according to jurisdiction. Understanding and complying with these requirements are essential for a successful career in law within any particular state.

10

TESTIMONIALS FROM LL.M. STUDENTS

Throughout this book, we have explored fundamental information for international lawyers seeking to study and practice in the United States. From the necessary steps to prepare academically and obtain a visa, to strategies for integrating into the U.S. legal market, we have provided a detailed and practical guide. However, beyond data and advice, there is an invaluable aspect that only LL.M. students can offer: their personal experiences.

In this chapter, we delve into the testimonials of those who have walked this path before. Each testimony not only offers a unique insight into individual challenges and triumphs but also reveals the emotions, obstacles overcome, and lessons learned during their journey in an LL.M. program in the United States. From initial adaptation to a new cultural and academic environment to the satisfaction of achieving significant academic and professional milestones, these narratives capture the essence of what it means to be an international law student in this country.

Exploring these testimonials not only provides inspiration but also offers a deeper understanding of the diverse paths LL.M. students can take. Each story reflects the diversity of professional and personal paths that international lawyers can pursue in the United States, highlighting the importance of effort, resilience, and determination in achieving educational and professional goals in a globalized and competitive legal environment.

The methodology for this chapter of LL.M. student testimonials is based on a series of questions designed to capture various perspectives and individual experiences. Each question seeks to delve into key aspects of students' experiences in the LL.M. program in the United States. Below is a detailed outline of how each question addresses different axes:

1. Motivation and University Selection: This question explores the student's initial motivations for pursuing an LL.M. in the United States and why they chose that particular university. It provides context on their goals and initial expectations.

2. Adaptation and Academic Challenges: Aimed at exploring both cultural adaptation and academic challenges within the program, this question allows students to share their experiences and the strategies used to overcome difficulties.

3. Resources and University Support: Seeks to identify the most useful resources and support within the university for international students, such as libraries, professional development offices, and student clubs.

4. Professional Development and Employment Advice: Focuses on the impact of the LL.M. program on the student's professional development and offers practical advice for job hunting in the United States.

5. Evaluation of Experience and Reflection: Invites students to reflect on the most valuable parts of their LL.M. experience and to share what they would change if they had the opportunity to repeat it, thus providing lessons learned for future students.

6. Bar Exam Preparation and School Support: This question focuses on how the LL.M. program prepared the student for the bar exam and what kind of support they received from the university during the preparation process, highlighting the importance of this critical aspect of legal education.

Each answer provides a unique perspective that enriches the overall understanding of the LL.M. experience in the United States, offering valuable advice and reflections that can guide other students on a similar path.

Yuntian Xia – China – LL.M. in National Security and Tech Law - Georgetown Law – 22 years old

I decided to pursue an LL.M. in the United States because in my country, it's almost impossible to find a good job without a master's degree. The top law universities in China require very high scores in a unified exam, which only the best students achieve. In contrast, to get into American law schools, you only need the TOEFL and a high GPA, besides tuition fees, which is much more accessible. Additionally, U.S. law schools allow you to take the NY Bar exam, a highly valued qualification in China. These were my more realistic reasons, but I also wanted to experience life in the United States and understand how this great empire works.

I chose Georgetown University because it's the best school in DC, and I wanted to be close to the heart of the United States. Living in DC for a year was an amazing experience.

Adapting to life in the United States was relatively easy. Most Chinese students quickly learn to cook and eat at home. However, the academic challenges were many. It's very difficult to learn law in a second language. In some J.D. classes, most of us needed to use a translator, and it was challenging to express our opinions, even to simple questions. It wasn't until the second semester that I began to adapt gradually. Within the university, I met a professor who provided me with a lot of help and personal guidance, answering many of my questions.

The LL.M. program gave me a solid understanding of the U.S. legal system and American society in general. I feel confident dealing with U.S.-related matters, not only in legal issues but also in finance or immigration matters. Finding a job in the United States is a difficult task for Chinese students due to international relations. Therefore, I recommend focusing on specific areas such as trade and immigration law, which may be more practical.

What I value most about my LL.M. experience is the opportunity to make friends from all over the world. As an organizer of Chinese students, I spent a lot of time communicating with my compatriots. If I had to do it again, I would choose a wider social network. Finally, I plan to take the NY Bar exam next semester, and the preparation I have received so far has been very helpful.

Jessica Silva – Brazil – LL.M. in International and Comparative Law – Cardozo School of Law – 29 years old

I had always wanted to move to the United States. In law school in Brazil, I focused my studies on international law, specifically human rights treaties. I planned to study something related to immigration and human rights. Since I applied late for fall applications, I only applied to Cardozo. I received a $25,000 scholarship (the total value of my LL.M. program is around $71,000). If I had more time, I would have applied to more schools, but I was happy with the scholarship I received.

Adapting to life in the United States was easier than I expected, as I have been visiting New York since I was 15 and knew how people lived here before arriving. Initially, in school, I used to get headaches after classes due to intensive exposure to English, but I got used to it. Introduction to U.S. Law was terrifying as I started learning about common law cases and how they differ from civil law. However, after a month, I was understanding everything quite well.

I still think cold calls are the worst. In classes with more J.D. students and a larger number of classmates, I asked not to participate in cold calls because I didn't want to speak in front of the class. However, there were some smaller classes where I liked to participate, which affected how the professors graded me.

The LL.M. program at Cardozo is well-developed. As they receive around 50 students per semester, they invest a lot in the LL.M. program. At the beginning of the course, we had many meetings with staff explaining the course, the library, online accounts (LexisNexis, etc.), how to use all the online tools the school offers, and how and with whom we could resolve various types of problems. There is a specific dean for LL.M. students with trained people to help us choose courses. If we have a problem with a professor, we can contact these people for help. I don't know any LL.M. student who hasn't passed any subject. They can get bad grades when they don't ask for help, but they never fail. The library is huge, and we can study there all day if we want. There are clubs, and LL.M. students are welcome to join, but the time we spend there is too short to get much exposure. I have some friends who joined the Latin American Law Students Association. I joined the immigration club, but there were only one or two events per semester.

There is a career development office at Cardozo. However, they don't help LL.M. students as much as J.D. students. They really help us write our resumes and LinkedIn profiles, but they hold job fairs at school for J.D. students and don't allow LL.M. students to participate. They even said that law firm offices aren't interested in LL.M. students for positions in the United States, and they couldn't help us. This was disrespectful because they sell the dream of studying and working in the United States, and then when we are finishing the course, they simply say that our background isn't welcome by law firm offices in the United States.

I can't yet answer how the LL.M. program has helped in my professional development because I'm still searching. What I can say is that I have an immigration student status that will allow me to work only one year (OPT). When applying for jobs, there is usually a question about the ability to work here in the United States permanently, and my answer is no. It's a challenge to even receive an interview invitation.

I greatly value the improvement in my legal writing skills and the comprehensive understanding I gained of the U.S. legal system during my LL.M. program. Additionally, the opportunity to make connections and build lasting friendships was incredibly rewarding. If I could do it again, I would conduct thorough market research to better understand the demands of the legal job market. This would allow me to select courses that align more closely with the skills and knowledge employers seek, thereby improving my job prospects.

I plan to take the bar exam in February 2025. In the first week of classes, the dean said that we should focus on buying a specific paid course for the bar exam because even J.D. students usually pay for it. The reason is that specific paid courses (like Barbri, Themis) are better equipped to train us for the exam. The support we received from the school was regarding the requirements for the application. They released a document with detailed instructions, which really helped. It taught us which subjects we needed to have on our resume, which subjects we needed to have on our resume, where we needed to apply, and everything else. However, the school did not provide any courses that taught the bar exam subjects.

Aylin Castillo – Ecuador – LL.M. in U.S. Legal Studies – St. John's University School of Law – 25 years old

My main motivation for pursuing an LL.M. in the United States has been to expand my knowledge in the U.S. legal field so I can help parts of the community that lack access to legal representation. I chose St. John's University because of its rigorous academic curriculum, personalized bar exam preparation support, and most importantly, the supportive environment provided by professors, academic staff, and peers.

Adapting to life in the United States and facing the academic challenges of the program has been quite a process. As a lawyer trained in a civil law country, confronting a completely different culture, educational system, and language has been a significant challenge, with some of these nuances often going unnoticed. The academic pressure of the program has forced me to push myself harder and adopt new habits, letting go of previous legal perspectives to adapt properly. However, it is immensely gratifying to continuously overcome these challenges because we are always learning; one never fully masters everything.

Within the LL.M. program, the most valuable support for me has been the professional development office, with whom I worked to perfect my resume and become a student ambassador for the LL.M. program at my school for the New York City Bar Association.

The LL.M. program has been fundamental to my professional development by providing me with a deep understanding of how to network effectively, develop application materials, prepare various types of legal documents, and other key aspects. My advice for future students seeking employment in the United States is to actively participate in clubs that align with their professional goals, attend networking events, and ensure they have a solid resume, because competition is high but not impossible to overcome.

What I value most about my LL.M. experience is the support received from both professors and academic staff; they always provide incredible feedback and motivation to keep going even during the toughest times. If I could repeat the program, I would focus more on actively participating in student clubs and making sure to interact more with J.D. students.

The LL.M. program at my school focuses heavily on bar exam preparation in various ways, such as offering a specific course that must be taken over two semesters, covering five main areas of the bar exam. Additionally, summer workshops are offered for additional bar exam areas, which students can use to strengthen their knowledge. Besides this, there is a lot of contact between professors and students in case there are specific questions about filing documentation with the BOLE and about the bar exam itself.

Mohammed Hamad Aldrees – Saudi Arabia – LL.M. in Intellectual Property – Boston University School of Law – 28 years old

I chose the United States primarily because of the variety and advancements they have achieved in the field of law, especially in intellectual property. I was very interested in this field, and that's why I decided to choose Boston University, as it is among the top ten law schools in this area.

Initially, I did not face major difficulties adapting to the culture, as I was aware of the cultural and ideological differences. However, the academic challenges were considerable. I clearly remember the enormous amount of reading required to prepare for classes and how difficult it was at first to keep up with the readings, especially reading in another language. Nevertheless, with time and effort, I managed to overcome this problem.

Most of the services provided by the university were very helpful, especially the library and law library services. Additionally, the university offered several introductory tours of the library and its services, which proved to be very beneficial.

Studying an LL.M. in the United States helped me immensely to understand the U.S. legal system and to prepare for the job market in this country. Therefore, my advice for new students is to focus primarily on studying the subjects for the U.S. bar exam if they wish to work here.

I have never wondered what I would change if I could go back in time because overall, my experience was very good. Studying law in another country with a different legal system helps to broaden your thoughts and strengthen your legal analysis. Additionally, meeting international students from other countries provides an invaluable cultural exchange. Studying abroad allowed me to meet people and friends from other countries, and in my opinion, this is one of the most important things gained from studying abroad. The beautiful and pleasant moments will become a cherished memory.

The university offered several meetings to introduce the bar exam and the basic requirements for each state. They also helped students become familiar with the available services to prepare for the exam. Moreover, the university helps set up a study schedule and prepares it for students who want to take the exam. They also provided a specialized service office for students who want to take the exam, helping them prepare their documents and keeping them informed about the necessary procedures.

11

REQUIREMENTS BY JURISDICTION

When considering the possibility of taking the bar exam in the United States after completing an LL.M., it is essential to understand that the requirements vary significantly from one jurisdiction to another. Each state establishes its own rules and conditions to allow international LL.M. graduates to take the exam.

The path to bar admission is not uniform and may involve several additional steps, such as meeting certain educational requirements, completing specific courses, or even obtaining a credential evaluation by local authorities. Some states are more receptive to international LL.M. graduates, offering a clearer and more direct path, while others may require additional training or impose stricter restrictions.

In this section, we will provide a detailed guide to the specific requirements by jurisdiction for LL.M. graduates who wish to take the bar exam. We will address states known to be more accessible to international graduates, as well as those with stricter requirements. We will also explore any additional regulations that may be relevant, such as practical experience requirements, the need to complete specific U.S. law modules, and variations in the format and content of the bar exam in each state.

Furthermore, we will discuss the importance of planning ahead and fully understanding the specific requirements and procedures of the jurisdiction in which you wish to practice. Knowing these differences can facilitate more effective planning and help avoid surprises during the bar admission process. This knowledge is crucial for aspiring lawyers who have completed or are considering an LL.M. program in the United States, as it allows them to prepare an appropriate strategy for their admission to legal practice in the state of their choice.[30]

Alabama

Applicants must meet and demonstrate the following requirements: (a) that the foreign law school from which they graduated is approved in the foreign jurisdiction where it is located; (b) that the applicant has been admitted to practice law in the jurisdiction in which the university or law school is located; and (c) at least one of the following conditions: (i) that the applicant's law degree program includes a substantial component of English common law; or (ii) that the applicant has successfully completed at least 24 semester hours of legal subjects covered by the bar exam in regular law school classes, under ABA standards; or (iii) that the applicant has been admitted to practice law before the highest court in a U.S. jurisdiction, has been continuously practicing law for at least 3 years in that jurisdiction, and is a member in good standing of the bar of that jurisdiction.

California

Graduates of foreign law schools must request an individual evaluation to determine the equivalence of their legal education. Foreign law school graduates may qualify to take the California bar exam if they obtain an LL.M. degree or complete an additional year of legal studies at an ABA-approved or California-accredited law school, which includes a certain number of credits in bar exam subjects. Foreign-educated law students who did not graduate are not eligible to take the exam and must obtain a J.D. degree at an ABA-approved or California-accredited law school or complete 4 years of legal studies at a registered California law school and pass the first-year law students' exam. Foreign law school graduates who are admitted to active legal practice in good standing in

---

[30] All requirements presented were adapted from the National Conference of Bar Examiners, available at https://reports.ncbex.org/comp-guide/charts/chart-4/#1610142352111-e56b1dc2-06b5

their countries do not need to complete additional legal studies to qualify to take the bar exam.

Colorado

Graduates of foreign law schools must request an individual evaluation to determine their eligibility to sit for the UBE in Colorado or transfer an eligible UBE score. A foreign-educated applicant has three paths to eligibility: (1) the applicant's foreign legal education is based on English common law principles that are substantially equivalent in duration to a U.S. J.D. education program, is in good standing and authorized to practice law in a foreign or other U.S. jurisdiction, and has been actively involved in legal practice for at least 3 of the last 5 years; (2) the applicant's foreign education is based on English common law principles that are substantially equivalent in duration to a U.S. J.D. education program and has completed an LL.M. degree at an ABA-accredited law school that meets certain curricular requirements; and (3) the applicant's foreign legal education is not based on English common law principles but is substantially equivalent in duration to a U.S. J.D. education program, is in good standing and authorized to practice law in a foreign or other U.S. jurisdiction, and has completed an LL.M. degree at an ABA-accredited law school that meets certain curricular requirements.

Connecticut

Graduates of foreign law schools must file a petition for the determination of foreign education and receive approval from the Bar Examining Committee before filing an application for admission by exam, admission without exam, or admission by UBE score transfer. Foreign education must be substantially equivalent in duration to the legal education provided by an ABA-approved law school. Foreign-educated applicants must complete an LL.M. degree program that meets specific requirements at an ABA-approved or Committee-approved law school before admission. An applicant who otherwise does not meet the educational requirements may be eligible to take the exam if certain conditions are met. These conditions include admission before the original highest court in a U.S. state, the District of Columbia, the Commonwealth of Puerto Rico, or a U.S. District Court for 10 years or more, being in good standing in that jurisdiction, and having actively practiced law in that jurisdiction for 5 of the last 7 years.

District of Columbia

Graduates of foreign law schools must have 3 years in good standing in another U.S. state or territory. Foreign law school graduates with less than 3 years of good standing admission in another U.S. state or territory must submit their foreign law degree transcripts for evaluation to determine if it is a qualifying degree and must also complete a minimum of 26 semester hours of study at a law school that at the time of such study was ABA-approved. All these semester hours must be obtained in single-subject courses in areas of law that are substantially tested on the Uniform Bar Exam. Classes that began before March 1, 2016, will count if they were in subjects tested on the DC bar exam until February 2016.

Florida

Applicants who have an LL.M. from an ABA-accredited law school that meets the board's curricular criteria can, after 2 years of active practice in another jurisdiction (District of Columbia or other U.S. states or in federal courts of the United States or its territories, possessions, or protectorates) in which the applicant has been duly admitted, submit a representative compilation of work for board evaluation. If the applicant does not have a qualifying LL.M., they must first practice law for 5 years in another jurisdiction as described above before being eligible to submit a representative compilation of work for review.

Georgia

A lawyer educated at a law school outside the United States may meet the educational requirements and be eligible to take the exam if the foreign-educated lawyer graduated from a foreign law school that meets the Rules' requirements; is authorized to practice law in the foreign jurisdiction; and has been awarded, by an ABA-approved law school, an LL.M. that meets the LL.M. Program's Curricular Criteria for Practice of Law in the United States adopted by the Board of Bar Examiners.

Illinois

The graduate of a foreign law school must have been authorized to practice in the country where the degree was awarded and/or in a U.S. jurisdiction for a minimum of 5 years; the lawyer must be in good standing as a lawyer or equivalent in that country or U.S. jurisdiction where they were admitted; for no less than 5 of the 7 years immediately preceding the application in Illinois, the lawyer must have verifiably dedicated a minimum of 1,000 hours annually to the practice of law in that country and/or U.S. jurisdiction where they are authorized; and the applicant must obtain a passing score on the MPRE and meet the character and fitness standards.

Maryland

A graduate of a foreign law school may qualify for a waiver to take the UBE in Maryland if they have been admitted by examination in another U.S. jurisdiction or have completed an additional degree at an ABA-approved law school where they have earned at least 26 credit hours in subjects tested on the UBE upon completion of the degree, except that the applicant may substitute up to 3 credit hours of Professional Responsibility in lieu of an equivalent number of UBE coursework hours.

Massachusetts

A graduate of a foreign law school (except for pre-approved Canadian law schools, as set forth in the Massachusetts Board of Bar Examiners Rule VI) may be allowed to file a petition for admission by examination after completing additional legal studies designated by the Board of Bar Examiners at an ABA-approved law school or a Massachusetts statute-approved law school. To apply for admission in Massachusetts, foreign-educated lawyers must demonstrate current eligibility to practice law in the foreign jurisdiction and obtain, in writing, a determination of educational sufficiency from the Board of Bar Examiners.

New York

The applicant must complete a period of law study equivalent in duration and substance to that specified in New York rules at a law school recognized by a competent accrediting agency of the foreign government. All applicants must have their transcripts evaluated by the Board of Law Examiners to determine if additional study is required in the form of a qualifying LL.M. degree from an ABA-approved law school in the United States.

Pennsylvania

The applicant must have completed law studies at a foreign law school, been admitted and in good standing with the bar association of a foreign jurisdiction, and practiced in that jurisdiction for 5 of the last 8 years. The applicant must also complete 24 credit hours in specified subjects at an ABA-approved law school.

Tennessee

A foreign-educated applicant has two paths to eligibility: one based solely on education and the other requiring education plus experience and an LL.M. degree in the U.S. An applicant is eligible solely based on education if their education is accredited by the relevant agency in the foreign country and is substantially equivalent to that required for U.S.-educated applicants (a bachelor's degree or higher and a J.D. degree obtained in one or more degrees in the foreign country). A full evaluation of educational equivalence for professional licensure by an organization that is a member of the National Association of Credential Evaluation Services must be provided to the Board with the application. If educational equivalence is not met, an applicant may be eligible if, in addition to foreign legal education at an accredited school, the applicant is licensed in the country where they were educated and has been actively engaged in the practice of law in that country for 5 of the 8 years preceding the application, and the applicant has been awarded an LL.M. from an ABA-accredited law school in the United States.

Texas

An applicant with an initial law degree from a foreign law school not based on English common law must be authorized to practice law and have a qualified LL.M. degree. An applicant with an initial law degree from a foreign law school based on English common law must have a qualified LL.M. degree or meet a 3-year practice requirement.

Vermont

A graduate of a foreign law school is eligible to take the bar exam if the applicant (1) has completed legal education at a foreign law school whose curriculum provided training in a system based on English common law and is otherwise equivalent to graduation from an approved law school, as determined by the equivalence determination process; and (2) has been admitted to the bar of a court of general jurisdiction in the country where the foreign law school is located and has maintained good standing in that bar or resigned from the bar while still in good standing.

Washington

An applicant with a foreign law degree that would qualify the applicant to practice law in that jurisdiction is eligible if they obtain an LL.M. "for the practice of law" from an ABA-accredited law school. The

LL.M. must meet the requirements of Washington's APR 3. However, foreign lawyers from English common law jurisdictions (with a law degree) are eligible without an LL.M. if they are currently admitted and have active legal experience in the common law jurisdiction for at least 3 of the 5 years immediately preceding the application.

The process for graduates of foreign law programs to become admitted attorneys in the United States varies significantly by jurisdiction. While some jurisdictions allow direct exam sitting after meeting certain educational and practice requirements, others require additional degrees, such as an LL.M., or validation of foreign legal education through equivalence assessments. Many other jurisdictions accept international lawyers under different conditions. Therefore, it is crucial to thoroughly research both the National Conference of Bar Examiners (NCBE) website and the relevant state authorities to understand specific and updated requirements. This includes obtaining additional degrees and practicing law, as well as familiarizing oneself with local bar admission rules and procedures. By doing so, aspiring lawyers can navigate the complex landscape of bar admission in the United States and effectively advance their legal careers.

12

CHECKLIST BEFORE THE FIRST DAY OF CLASSES

Preparing adequately before the first day of classes is crucial to ensure a smooth transition and a successful start to your LL.M. program in the United States. From selecting the right program to understanding the differences in legal systems and preparing financially, each step is essential to maximize your educational and professional experience.

This detailed checklist is designed to guide you through all the stages we've previously discussed, providing a clear and organized path to ensure you don't get lost in the process. It includes initial steps like researching and applying to programs, obtaining a student visa, managing finances, and academic and ethical preparation. By following this checklist, you can ensure that you are ready to face the challenges and make the most of the opportunities your LL.M. program offers.

- ☐ Read the survival guide for foreign attorneys to have legal success practicing law in the United States.
- ☐ Analyze the different available programs and make a list of universities you want to apply to.
- ☐ Research the admission requirements of the universities you are interested in and gather the necessary documentation.

- ☐ Complete the Form I-20 application with the International Student Office of the university you finally decide to attend.
- ☐ Pay the SEVIS fee.
- ☐ Schedule an appointment at the corresponding embassy and apply for the F-1 visa.
- ☐ Attend the embassy appointment for an interview with a consular officer.
- ☐ Purchase your plane ticket to the United States and organize the necessary documentation.
- ☐ Organize finances and sources of income to cover tuition and living costs.
- ☐ Select the courses to study in the first semester.
- ☐ Send your vaccination records to the university if necessary.
- ☐ Participate in English for American Law School classes.
- ☐ Practice the IRAC method of legal writing and reading legal texts.
- ☐ Review the application requirements for international lawyers in the jurisdiction you wish to apply to.
- ☐ Apply for a prior education evaluation with the Board of Law Examiners of the jurisdiction you wish to apply to.
- ☐ Review the syllabi of the chosen courses and complete the readings and assignments for the first week.
- ☐ Attend the law school's introduction week.
- ☐ Enjoy the experience to the fullest!

By following these steps in detail, you not only ensure that you meet all the prerequisites, but you also prepare yourself mentally and emotionally for the challenges ahead. Each stage of this process is fundamental to building a solid foundation that will allow you to make the most of your educational and professional experience in the United States.

Remember that the key to a successful start is being well-informed and prepared. Use this checklist as a comprehensive guide to ensure you don't miss any important details. With proper preparation, you willp be ready to face and overcome any obstacles and stand out in your LL.M. program.

Good luck on your new academic and professional adventure!

13

ADDITIONAL RESOURCES

In this section, we will provide a list of additional resources that can be very useful for international LL.M. students. These resources range from online tools to professional organizations and university services, designed to help students navigate their educational and professional experiences in the United States. The information presented here can complement the knowledge acquired in classes and facilitate the process of adapting to a new academic and cultural environment.

Professional Organizations and Associations

1. American Bar Association (ABA)

   - **Description:** The ABA is one of the largest and most prestigious lawyer associations in the United States. It offers a wide range of resources, including publications, continuing education programs, and networking opportunities.
   - **Website:** www.americanbar.org

2. National Association for Law Placement (NALP)

   - **Description:** NALP provides resources for legal career planning and offers information on employment trends in the legal sector.
   - **Website:** www.nalp.org

3. International Bar Association (IBA)

- **Description:** The IBA connects lawyers worldwide and provides global resources, events, and publications for legal professionals.
  - **Website:** www.ibanet.org
4. Hispanic National Bar Association (HNBA)
  - **Description:** The HNBA represents the interests of Hispanic lawyers in the United States, offering resources, networking, and professional support to its members.
  - **Website:** www.hnba.com
5. Dominican Bar Association (DBA)
  - **Description:** The DBA supports lawyers of Dominican descent and other legal professionals, promoting diversity and offering resources and networking opportunities.
  - **Website:** www.dominicanbarassociation.org

Recommended Books and Publications

1. "Black's Law Dictionary"
  - **Description:** Considered the most comprehensive and authoritative legal dictionary in the United States. It is an indispensable tool for any law student.
2. "Getting to Maybe: How to Excel on Law School Exams" by Richard Michael Fischl and Jeremy Paul
  - **Description:** This book provides strategies and techniques for succeeding in law school exams.
3. Law Reviews
  - **Description:** Academic publications edited by students that offer articles on a variety of current legal topics.
4. "1001 Legal Words"
  - **Description:** An essential resource for international students, this book helps understand legal vocabulary in English.
5. Bluebook Citation, 21st ed.
  - **Description:** The standard reference guide for legal citation in the United States.
6. "E. Allan Farnsworth: Introduction to the Legal System of the United States"
  - **Description:** A fundamental text that offers an overview of the U.S. legal system.
7. "The Lawyer's Craft: An Introduction to Legal Analysis, Writing, Research, and Advocacy"

- **Description**: A book focusing on practical skills and the craft of law.
8. The Indigo Book
- **Description:** A free online resource offering an open citation guide.
9. "A Short and Happy Guide" Series
- **Description:** A series of books offering concise and easy-to-understand guides on various legal topics, ideal for students seeking a quick and clear understanding of complex concepts.
10. "Academic Legal Discourse and Analysis: Essential Skills for International Students Studying Law in The United States"
- **Description:** Designed specifically for international students studying law in the United States, this book provides essential skills for understanding and participating in academic legal discourse in the U.S. context, facilitating transition and success in legal studies.

Important Regulations

1. Model Rules of Professional Conduct (MRPC)
- **Description:** The MRPC are the model rules of professional conduct developed by the American Bar Association (ABA) and serve as the basis for ethical standards in many U.S. jurisdictions.
- **Website:**
www.americanbar.org/groups/professional_responsibility/publications/model_rules_of_professional_conduct/model_rules_of_professional_conduct_table_of_contents/
2. Federal Rules of Evidence (FRE)
- **Description:** A set of rules governing the admissibility of evidence in U.S. federal courts.
- **Website:** www.law.cornell.edu/rules/fre
3. Federal Rules of Civil Procedure (FRCP)
- **Description:** The FRCP are the rules that govern procedures in U.S. federal civil courts.
- **Website:** www.law.cornell.edu/rules/frcp

Online Resources

1. Westlaw and LexisNexis
- **Description:** These legal databases offer access to a vast amount of case law, legislation, and academic articles. They are essential tools for legal research.

- **Websites:** legal.thomsonreuters.com/en/westlaw, www.lexisnexis.com

2. Beyond Non-J.D.: LL.M. Webpage

- **Description:** A platform dedicated to providing specific information and resources for LL.M. students.
- **Website:** beyondnonjd.wordpress.com/

3. Cornell Legal Information Institute (LII)

- **Description:** An online resource offering detailed definitions and explanations of legal terms.
- **Website:** www.law.cornell.edu

4. US Law Essentials

- **Description:** A website offering educational resources on U.S. law, particularly useful for international students.
- **Website:** www.uslawessentials.com

Available Resources at the University

1. Law Library

- **Description:** University law libraries typically offer access to legal databases, book collections, and research assistance.

2. Offices of Diversity, Equity, and Inclusion (DEI)

- **Description:** They provide support and resources for students from diverse backgrounds and promote an inclusive environment on campus.

3. Career Development Office (CDO)

- **Description:** Offers career guidance services, including job search workshops, resume reviews, and interview preparation.

4. Academic and Wellness Advisors

- **Description:** Provide emotional support and guidance to help students manage stress and other personal and academic challenges.

5. Law Reviews and Journals

- **Description:** Participating in law reviews offers experience in legal research and writing, and is an excellent opportunity for professional development.

6. Student Clubs and Societies

- **Description:** Involvement in law-related clubs provides networking opportunities and skill development outside the classroom.

7. Legal Writing and Tutoring Centers

- **Description:** Many universities offer academic support centers where students can get help with legal writing and other essential skills.

Financial Resources

1. Scholarships.com

- **Description:** An online database that helps students find available scholarships and financial aid.
- **Website:** www.scholarships.com

2. FAFSA (Free Application for Federal Student Aid)

- **Description:** While most international students are not eligible for federal aid, completing the FAFSA can be useful for certain types of scholarships and loans.
- Website: www.fafsa.ed.gov

Time Management and Productivity Tools

1. Todoist

- Description: A task management app that helps organize and prioritize academic and personal work.
- **Website**: www.todoist.com

2. Trello

- **Description:** A project management tool based on boards that facilitates collaboration and task planning.
- **Website:** www.trello.com

3. Google Calendar

- **Description:** A digital calendar tool that allows scheduling and reminders for important events, meetings, and deadlines.
- **Website:** calendar.google.com

Having access to a variety of additional resources can make a significant difference in the experience of an international LL.M. student. Utilizing these tools and organizations will not only help improve academic performance but also facilitate integration into the U.S. legal community. Be sure to explore and use these resources to maximize your potential and achieve your educational and professional goals.

EPILOGUE:
TOWARDS A GLOBAL AND
INCLUSIVE LEGAL COMMUNITY

After evaluating everything presented in this book, including cultural adaptation, the necessary exams, and integration into the job market, it is clear that foreign lawyers face a series of significant challenges. Adapting to a new environment, overcoming rigorous exams, and being valued in the U.S. job market is no easy task. Cultural differences, language barriers, and the need to understand a different legal system add layers of complexity that require effort and dedication.

LL.M. programs offer an invaluable opportunity for foreign lawyers to integrate into the U.S. legal system. However, the journey does not end with obtaining the degree. International lawyers face a challenging path in seeking job opportunities and gaining acceptance in the U.S. legal community.

It is crucial for international lawyers to come together and create a legal community where they support each other and seek mutual growth. This support network can provide the emotional and professional backing needed to navigate these challenges. Sharing resources, experiences, and advice is fundamental to overcoming obstacles. Additionally, providing support in exam preparation and job searches can make a significant difference in the professional success of each community member.

Raising awareness within the entire legal community about the significance and value of LL.M. programs is also essential to keep opening doors for foreign lawyers. Those in leadership positions should prioritize hiring candidates with an international background. The diversity of perspectives brought by international lawyers can greatly enrich legal practice and problem-solving. Often, companies avoid hiring F-1 OPT students to avoid the H1-B visa sponsorship process. Therefore, collaboration among colleagues and community support are essential to overcoming these barriers.

Moreover, it is vital to form support groups for bar preparation, organize to demand more transparency in pass rates, and develop programs more focused on LL.M. students. Joint bar preparation can significantly increase success rates and help international lawyers meet the requirements to practice in the United States.

Additionally, we must advocate together to ensure that more jurisdictions accept international prospects and that requirements become more accessible. Collaboration and mutual support are fundamental to overcoming these challenges and ensuring that foreign lawyers can fully contribute to the U.S. legal community. Creating a global legal community benefits international lawyers and enriches the legal profession as a whole. Through mutual support and joint advocacy, we can achieve a more inclusive and accessible environment for all lawyers, regardless of their origin.

The success stories of those who have successfully integrated into the U.S. job market remind us that, although the path is arduous, it is attainable. Looking to the future, we envision a legal profession that values and leverages diversity and international experiences, enriching the practice of law and legal problem-solving on a global scale. With resilience, perseverance, and a supportive community, international lawyers can not only overcome challenges but also contribute significantly to the field of law in the United States.

ABOUT THE AUTHOR

Maike Miguel Lara Espinal, born on January 25, 2002, in Santo Domingo, Dominican Republic, is a distinguished legal scholar with an outstanding academic and professional track record. He completed his LL.M. in Transnational Legal Practice at St. John's University School of Law, graduating as Valedictorian in May 2024. During his time at St. John's, Maike was recognized with multiple scholarships and awards, including the Saavedra Family Scholarship awarded by the Dominican Bar Association in 2023, and several Dean's Excellence Awards in International Law, Business Organizations, Legal Writing II, and Applied Legal Analysis.

He has worked as a law clerk in the New York State Assembly, collaborating with Assemblymen Jake Blumencranz and George Alvarez, where he led legal and legislative research initiatives. He also served as the international programs coordinator at the Ministry of Education of the Dominican Republic, overseeing the coordination of international projects. At the Inter-American Telecommunications Commission of the OAS, he evaluated legal and regulatory frameworks in Latin America.

Maike has authored various publications in legal journals, including "The Need to Promote Technical-Scientific Diplomacy in Central America and the Caribbean" and "The Escalation of the Ukraine-Russia Conflict: Towards a New Paradigm in Human Rights." His latest article for the New York International Law Review is awaiting publication. He has represented the Dominican Republic in numerous international forums, including the 52nd OAS General Assembly in Lima, Peru, the 9th Summit of the Americas in Los Angeles, CA, and the 10th World Bank Youth Summit in Washington, D.C.

Fluent in Spanish, English, and French, Maike is a passionate advocate for the role of international students in LL.M. programs in the United States. His commitment to social justice and human rights, combined with his international and academic experience, makes him a highly skilled professional dedicated to promoting a fair and equitable legal framework globally.

Made in the USA
Columbia, SC
01 October 2024

42570588R00089